D0308323

PARK LEARNING CENTRE
The Park Cheltenham
Gloucestershire GL50 2RH
Telephone: 01242 714333

UNIVERSITY OF
GLOUCESTERSHIRE
at Cheltenham and Gloucester

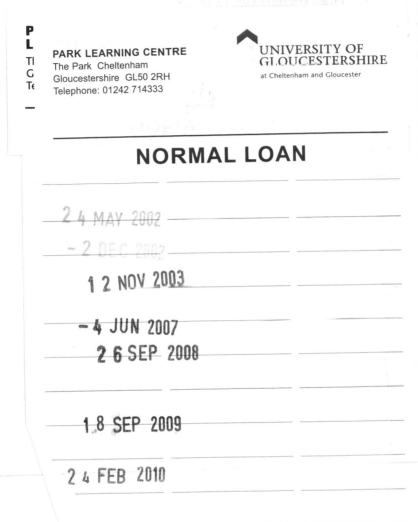

NORMAL LOAN

2 4 MAY 2002

- 2 DEC 2002

1 2 NOV 2003

- 4 JUN 2007

2 6 SEP 2008

1 8 SEP 2009

2 4 FEB 2010

The Uses and Misuses of Data and Models

The Mathematization of the Human Sciences

PARK LEARNING CENTRE
UNIVERSITY OF GLOUCESTERSHIRE
PO Box 220, The Park, Cheltenham, GL50 2QF
Tel: (01242) 532721

W. James Bradley
Kurt C. Schaefer

SAGE Publications
International Educational and Professional Publisher
Thousand Oaks   London   New Delhi

Copyright © 1998 by Sage Publications, Inc.

All rights reserved. No part of this book may be reproduced or utilized in any form or by any means, electronic or mechanical, including photocopying, recording, or by any information storage and retrieval system, without permission in writing from the publisher.

For information:

SAGE Publications, Inc.
2455 Teller Road
Thousand Oaks, California 91320
E-mail@sagepub.com

SAGE Publications Ltd.
6 Bonhill Street
London EC2A 4PU
United Kingdom

SAGE Publications India Pvt. Ltd.
M-32 Market
Greater Kailash I
New Delhi 110048 India

Printed in the United States of America

Library of Congress Cataloging-in-Publication Data

Bradley, James, 1943-
    The uses and misuses of data and models : The mathematization
of the human sciences / by W. James Bradley and Kurt C. Schaefer.
    p. cm.
    Includes bibliographical references and index.
    ISBN 0-7619-0921-4 (cloth : acid-free paper)
    ISBN 0-7619-0922-2 (pbk. : acid-free paper)
    1. Social sciences—Mathematical models. 2. Social
sciences—Statistical methods. 3. Social sciences—Methodology. I.
Schaefer, Kurt. C. II. Title.
    H61.25 .B69 1998
    300'.1'51—ddc21   98-9037

98 99 00 01 02 03 04 8 7 6 5 4 3 2 1

Acquiring Editor:	Peter Labella
Production Editor:	Wendy Westgate
Editorial Assistant:	Denise Santoya
Typesetter/Designer:	Danielle Dillahunt
Indexer:	Teri Greenberg
Cover Designer:	Ravi Balasuriya

Contents

Preface

One of the most influential books written in the social sciences in the 20th century is *The Theory of Games and Economic Behavior* by John von Neumann and Oskar Morgenstern (1937, 1946, 1953). In the first chapter, von Neumann and Morgenstern asked why mathematics has not been as successful in economics as it has been in physics, chemistry, and biology. They argued against several commonly offered reasons, such as the presence of psychological factors in economics, the absence of measurements of some important factors, and the discrete nature of economic quantities. They concluded that "the reason why mathematics has not been more successful must, consequently, be found elsewhere. The lack of real success is largely due to a combination of unfavorable circumstances, some of which can be removed gradually" (p. 4).

The unfavorable circumstances they listed were that "economic problems were not formulated clearly," the "mathematical tools were seldom used appropriately," and "the empirical background of economic science is definitely inadequate." Thus, von Neumann and Morgenstern laid out their vision of a mature discipline of economics, characterized by careful empirical observation, precisely formulated questions, and the fruitful use of appropriate mathematics. Such a vision has stimulated and shaped much work in all of the social sciences, not just economics, before and since von Neumann and Morgenstern's book was published.

The authors of this book are in many ways intellectual descendants of von Neumann and Morgenstern. One of us was trained as an econometrician and one as a mathematician with a dissertation in game theory. Both of us have spent our careers as teachers and practitioners of mathematical methods in the social and human sciences. Thus, we hold these methods in high regard.

But we also have some growing concerns about the approach that von Neumann and Morgenstern's vision represents. Our concerns have culminated in the writing of this book. Some specific events and circumstances that have contributed to our concerns are the following:

■ *The amount of "human information" in our culture—that is, data and summaries of data derived directly from or about individual human beings, communities, and institutions—has increased rapidly in recent years.* These data stem from IQ tests, polling, customer satisfaction surveys, indexes of the quality of life in various communities, and a myriad of other measures. Such data are used to make major decisions regarding people's education, employment, and place of residence, and they exercise a major influence on business decisions and governmental policies. Because such decisions are so important, researchers and practitioners have a significant responsibility to see that such data are accurate, meaningful, and are presented in such a way that they contribute to good decision making.

■ *The increased volume of human information has made the question "Ought data about human beings to be regarded in the same fashion as data that arise in the natural sciences?" more critical.* One difference is that data about humans have the potential to alter the persons about whom the data have been collected and their relationships with other persons. The study and application of human data never can be separated from ethical issues.

■ *Several critiques of science have recently been advanced.* Thomas Kuhn, Karl Popper, and other philosophers of science have argued that science occurs in a cultural context and that scientists are never wholly "objective." Their work has been followed by a number of "post modern" critiques of science, all of which might influence the way one practices social science. As a result, a polarization often is found in the social sciences between "positivists" and "interpretivists." Positivists focus on what can be observed; although they might acknowledge insights from writers like Kuhn and Popper, their practice often does not reflect these insights. Interpretivists often avoid the use of numbers, and insist on including "unobservables" in their analyses. The most notable unobservable advocated is speculation on the purposes and motivations of individuals and communities.

■ *The discussion of norms, values, and purpose often is omitted from much social research, especially by those who work in the positivist framework.* This omission is often well-intentioned: Scholars seek to develop transferrable knowledge—knowledge that is not dependent on individual opinion, perspective, or preference. But science has implicit norms and often is used in a context in which normative considerations are necessary. So, discussion of the appropriate role for norms, values, and purposes is needed.

■ *Training in the collection and use of human information often is too narrow.* Information begins with the formulation of a question and the belief that data can help answer it. It continues through collection of that data, and ultimately leads to decisions made and/or policies formed on the basis of those data. Some scholars specialize in understanding the philosophical issues underlying the formulation of questions and the selection of methods, others in the technical dimensions of data gathering and analysis, others in policy formation or decision making. But few people seem to have a perspective on the whole process. Thus, each acts within a narrow context; an improvement from the perspective of a limited frame of reference may not really improve the whole.

Our goal in this book is to develop principles that can guide the use of data and models in the social and decision sciences. In the process we will address each of the preceding concerns. Our intended audiences are researchers and practitioners in the social and decision sciences, decision makers, and students preparing for these fields. For those currently using mathematical, empirical, or both methods, we hope this book will challenge them to rethink their use. For nonusers, we hope this book will provide a challenge to reconsider. Perhaps their rejection of these methods has been based on experiences of inappropriate use.

We write as scholars who are at home with empirical and mathematical social science, yet who are trying to take seriously the many legitimate critiques of this heritage. Specifically, we believe that it is possible for our disciplines to work at developing norms without becoming radically subjective. Our hope is that this book will serve as one example of how this kind of analysis can be done.

There are three main themes in this book. The first is an attempt at understanding our times. What is special about this moment in time for people interested in the use of data and models in the social and human sciences? The second is the theme that norms, values, and purpose need to become a standard part of the work of people in the social and decision sciences. Without daily consideration of norms, values, and purpose, important facets of our work are neglected. And third, we hope to show that consideration of norms, values, and purpose can provide broad social benefits and help us to avoid doing harm.

This book was written with the financial support of the Calvin Center for Christian Scholarship. We would like to thank the center, its director, Ronald Wells, and its staff, Donna Romanowski and Kate Miller, for that support. Without the encouragement and assistance of all three of them, this work would have been much more difficult and a lot less enjoyable. We would also like to thank five reviewers we know for their helpful comments: Marvin Bolt, Walter Bradley, John Edelman, John Mason, and Allen Shoemaker, as well as two anonymous reviewers engaged by Sage Publications. We would also like to thank Peter Labella of Sage for his support and helpful critiques of early drafts of the manuscript. We are also grateful for the support and patience of our spouses, Anne Schaefer and Hope Bradley.

PART I

FOUNDATIONS

Our goal for Part I is to introduce and establish a context for the question, "What principles ought to guide the use of data and models in the social and decision sciences?"

Chapter 1 clarifies our question. It shows why it is important by demonstrating how widespread the use of human information has become and by discussing several problems that have arisen in its use. It also presents the approaches we will use to address this question. Chapter 2 discusses the concept of model because so much of what we subsequently say depends on the nature of models and the modeling process, we have set aside this chapter to focus on modeling. And Chapter 3 places our question in its historical context.

Our goal for Part II is to develop the guiding principles.

Oracles, Norms, and Science

Herodotus's *History of Ancient Greece* tells of King Croesus's deep concerns about the growing power of the Persians. He wanted to attack but decided first to consult several oracles—priests and priestesses believed capable of speaking under divine inspiration. So he sent messengers with the instruction that they were to approach each oracle on precisely the 100th day after being sent. They were simply to ask what Croesus was doing on that day; Croesus had arranged that on the 100th day he would chop up a tortoise and some lamb's meat and boil them together in a bronze cauldron with a bronze lid on it. At the moment his messengers entered the great hall at Delphi, the priestesses said, "A smell steals over my senses, the smell of a hard-shelled tortoise, seethed in bronze with the meat of lambs, mingled together; bronze is the base beneath, and bronze the vestment upon it" (Rawlinson, 1932).

Hearing of this, Croesus decided that the oracle of Delphi was the only true oracle. He burned offerings to Apollo, the god of Delphi, of 3,000 of each kind of sacrificial animal. He gave enormous quantities of gold and two huge mixing bowls, one of gold and one of silver, along with other gifts. He then sent his messengers again, this time with a different question.

3

"Shall Croesus make war upon the Persians?" The oracles answered that if he made war upon the Persians he would destroy a mighty empire. Croesus was overjoyed with this response but did not grasp that the empire referred to was his own (Rawlinson, 1932).

Croesus is a metaphor for our age. We, too, seek wisdom before we make decisions. But for us, scientific methodology serves the same role the oracles served for Croesus. We have tested this modern oracle and discovered that it has given many accurate responses to our questions; thus, we have developed confidence in it. We have invested a great deal of wealth in developing the oracle. And it has given us much information in return. But information is different from wisdom, as Croesus illustrates. Having enormous quantities of information at our fingertips does not ensure that we understand our world or that we make better decisions than our forebearers. In fact, information can provide an illusion of wisdom that renders us less wise than we would have been without it.

But more information does not *necessarily* make us less wise—Croesus had the answer he sought, but he did not interpret it properly. And neither can we naively ask questions of science without some principles to guide us in formulating our questions and in understanding how to interpret the answers we receive.

THE PURPOSE OF THIS BOOK

Our era is called "The Information Age." We shall take the word *information* as referring to data and any summaries or inferences derived from data. Our particular concern here is with one class of information and how it is developed: information about human beings and human institutions, the type of information produced by the social and decision sciences. We see much good but also much potential for confusion, misunderstanding, and harm arising from the use of human information. Such harm is not inevitable, but the development and handling of human information require care and understanding if harms are to be avoided.

Several terms describe the methods of generating information we want to discuss here. The words *positive* or *positivistic* are sometimes used to suggest empirical approaches that employ careful observation and measurement and avoid speculative interpretation. Nevertheless, positivism has fallen into disrepute since the mid-1960s for reasons we will discuss in some detail in Chapter 3. *Formal methods* or *formalism* are sometimes used, but these words tend to suggest methods that are primarily mathematical and in which the mode of persuasion is mathematical proof rather than empirical investigation. *Quantitative methods* probably comes closest to what we want to discuss, but not all social science data are numerical (for example, the identification of social class). The phrase *quantitative methods* also is often associated with methods that are highly statistical; although that is part of what we are addressing, many important models in the social and decision sciences are not based on statistics.

In essence, we want to address the methods of "social *science*" as contrasted with "social *studies*" (which include many methods that are not scientific). But the phrase *social science* has become virtually a synonym for social studies, so this phrase doesn't convey the meaning we want either. Thus, rather than use any of these terms, we simply refer to the "use of data and models in the social sciences." Although this phrase may seem a bit bland, it has the decided advantage of simply naming the tools we are interested in without any of the associations that accompany the other terms.

Our purpose, then, is to address the question "What principles ought to guide the development and use of data and models in the social sciences?" We will not be presenting and explaining social science methods in this book unless needed to prepare for discussion of a principle; there are many excellent books that present these methods.

In the next section, we illustrate how widespread human information has become so that we can see how greatly such principles are needed.

THE SCOPE OF HUMAN INFORMATION

We are all familiar with some common examples of seeking social benefits with data and models. Intelligence tests and personality inventories are routinely used to recommend career tracks for children and adults in hiring and occasionally in job assignments. The distribution of seats in Congress and the allocation of money by various federal-funding programs is based on census data. Extensive market research is often done before money is invested in the development of new products. But these examples are only the tip of the proverbial iceberg. In this section we will see several examples that demonstrate the large quantity of human information that is available.

The Inter-University Consortium for Political and Social Research (ICPSR) provides an archive for social science data. Here is how ICPSR describes its holdings.

Beginning with a few major surveys of the American electorate, the holdings of the archive have now broadened to include comparable information from diverse settings and for extended time periods. Data ranging from nine-teenth century French census materials to recent sessions of the United Nations, from American elections in the 1790s to the socioeconomic structure of Polish poviats, from the characteristics of Knights of Labor assemblies to the expectations of American consumers are included in the archive. Surveys, aggregate data, and computer based teaching packages in various substantive areas are continually deposited in the archive by leading scholars around the world. . . . The content of the archive extends across economic, sociological, historical, organizational, social, psychological, and political concerns. . . . Topical expansion is taking place to include urban studies, education, electoral behavior, socialization, foreign policy, commu-nity studies, judicial behavior, legislators (national, state, and local), race relations, and organizational behavior.[1]

The ICPSR maintains a database containing data from 2,900 distinct study titles and this database grows at the rate of roughly 200 titles per year. It also maintains the complete text of questions asked in selected surveys and provides means to search the actual question text. All of this is available via the Internet.

Much human data are collected via mental measurements. For instance, the 11th edition of *Buros' Mental Measurement Handbook*[2] contains a bibliography of 477 commercially available tests published in either new or revised form between 1989 and 1992 as well as 703 test reviews. Table 1.1 tabulates these tests by area. There is no way to determine the frequency of application of each of these tests, but some frequencies are known. In 1941, for example, 11,000 students took the Scholastic Aptitude Test (SAT); in 1994, about 1.25 million high school students took the SAT test. Many college admissions personnel (especially at selective colleges and universities) use SAT scores to help them make admissions decisions. Also in 1994, another 1.5 million sophomores and juniors took the PSAT/NMSQT (Preliminary Scholastic Aptitude Test / National Merit Scholarship Quali-fying Test); National Merit Scholars are selected based on the results of this test. The Weschler Adult Intelligence Survey (WAIS) and the Weschler Intelligence Survey for Children (WISC) also are widely used. For instance, *Tests in Print IV*[3] lists 1,131 articles referencing the WAIS test. Guidance and career counselors use the WAIS to help children, college students, and adults select programs of study and make career plans. The American armed forces administers the Armed Forces Qualification Test (which is

TABLE 1.1 Mental Tests by Major Classifications

Classification	Number	Percent
Personality	135	28.3
Vocations	84	17.6
Developmental	33	6.9
English	32	6.7
Education	29	6.1
Miscellaneous	29	6.1
Achievement	22	4.6
Intelligence and Scholastic Aptitude	22	4.6
Reading	21	4.4
Speech and Hearing	20	4.2
Mathematics	14	2.9
Neuropsychological	14	2.9
Behavior assessment	10	2.1
Sensory-Motor	6	1.3
Science	2	0.4
Social Studies	2	0.4
Fine Arts	1	0.2
Multiaptitude Batteries	1	0.2
Total	477	100

explicitly an intelligence test) to all of its members. The Myers-Briggs test measures the way people interact with others—it is widely used in professional training, career counseling, team building, and even marriage counseling to help people gain self-understanding. For instance, a popular recent publication[4] attempts to advise readers on their career selections based on their Myers-Briggs test results.

Human data collection does not end with mental measurements. In economics, the use of data, analysis founded on data, and mathematical models (which may or may not be based on data) also has grown. In Figure 1.1, we present a chart showing the growth of the pages published in the field of mathematical economics between 1944 and 1977.

In business, we see other dimensions of the use of human information. For instance, a human resources or payroll system used by many American businesses allows employers to maintain extensive information about employees, including retirement plans and amounts, languages spoken, bank account numbers, beneficiaries, marital status, benefits, charitable

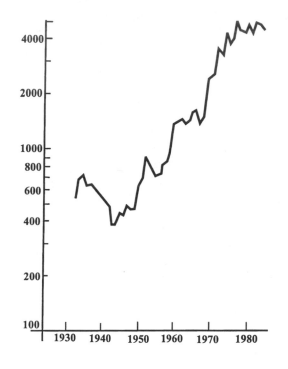

Figure 1.1.

withholdings, use of a company car, education, disability, dependents, experience, amount of pay garnished, pay history, job evaluation history, previous job, deductions, the issuance of company equipment, and circumstances surrounding termination.

Personnel data are only one aspect of the data collected by businesses. Enormous quantities of accounting data normally are maintained. There are also market research data, data on the economic climate, competitors, sales, and various aspects of productivity.

These are just a few examples. In fact, it's hard to even pick up a newspaper without encountering significant amounts of human information. For example, in a recent issue[5] of the newspaper *USA Today,* in the first section alone, data were presented on frequency of air travel, funds raised by political candidates, United Nations votes, attendance at an ice-fishing competition, mortgage rates, growth in the number of words in the Internal Revenue Code and Regulations during 40 years, anticipated profits from a book by John Hinkley (convicted of attempting to assassinate then-President Ronald Reagan), the proportion of American donut shops that ban smoking, the value and nature of Chinese imports to the United States, federal budget cuts, a survey of perceptions of the Smithsonian Institute, the training of Army Rangers, the transplant of Canadian gray wolves to Yellowstone Park, frequency of flight delays, the costs of the O. J. Simpson trial, congressional ethics charges, the United Nations withdrawal from Somalia, the size of U.S. forces in Haiti, rates of growth of selected airports, alleged Iraqi oil smuggling, and government subsidization of water distribution in the western United States.

In summary, an enormous quantity of human information is currently being developed and used. Because there is so much human information, the potential for its misuse poses significant risks. In the next four sections we examine some potential problems.[6]

PROBLEMS IN GATHERING HUMAN INFORMATION

Methodological Problems

Our first set of problems arises because the assumptions inherent in a methodology originally developed for the natural sciences may not always apply to the study of human beings and human institutions. Traditionally, the (scientific) methods we want to address here have been characterized by

- careful observation,
- measurement,
- the use of symbolic representations of entities and relationships (i.e., models),
- mathematical analysis of these models,
- a focus on replicable events,
- Occam's razor (focusing on aspects of phenomena judged to be essential and ignoring other aspects)—that is, intentional separation of observations from context,
- the search for patterns (or laws) expressed mathematically,
- attempts to find causal explanations.

But there are also several activities that social scientists have sought to avoid, at least within their work as social scientists. Among these are

- interpretation of cultural or historical trends in light of a worldview or hermeneutical scheme,
- judgments of right or wrong,
- advocacy of causes or points of view.

Thus, the "ideal" social scientist traditionally has been a "disinterested" (but not uninterested) observer of human affairs, reporting on them carefully and accurately but neither judging human actions nor advocating his or her own perspective.

But the characteristics listed above do not necessarily apply to social science. Consider the notion of reproducible results.[7] Human events, such as the particular economic conditions of one quarter, never can be duplicated. Similarly, we cannot say, "Let's rerun Napoleon's Russian campaign with different assumptions and see what happens." Also, consider Occam's razor. When applied to human individuals, groups, or institutions, it requires one to ignore the holistic nature of human beings and to separate data from context. For human beings, the whole is more than the sum of the parts; the identity of an individual, group, or institution is found in its totality and the context in which it is embedded. Thus, attempts to use methods borrowed from the world of replicable results separated from context may be fruitful in some ways, but they necessarily misrepresent the human situation.

Second, the scientific notion of the disinterested observer who simply reports the facts has been questioned in the light of recent advances. Philosophers of science have pointed out that what we observe may depend as much on the prior understandings we bring to an observation as on the object observed. This critique applies to all of science but is particularly acute in the social sciences. For example, suppose you are visiting the home of a new friend—you have not been there before. He invites you to join him on the porch. As you walk on the porch, your eyes fall on a chaise lounge. Note what has happened here: you observe a chaise lounge, not a collection of photons striking your retina. That is, your very act of observation is an act of interpretation. Consider a person from a different cultural background who had never seen a chaise lounge. She would not make the same observation; in fact, she might well ask "What is that?" expressing her inability to interpret what her senses are reporting. Such deeply rooted entanglements of observer and observed are abundant in the social sciences. For instance, consider an anthropologist attempting to observe the patterns of interaction in a particular community. What features the anthropologist observes depend heavily on the categories the anthropologist brings to the act of observation. Thus, *observations* are "theory-laden"; that is, it is impossible to avoid the kind of *a priori* assumptions and cultural influences that our ideal scientist sought to exclude.

There are more difficulties. Here are some: Social science data often lack the precision of natural science data but may be regarded as if they have that precision. Critically important concepts may resist precise definition. Human beings and their circumstances are extremely complex, so scientific analysis typically requires major simplifications and idealizations. Human intentionality may introduce nonreplicability. Controlled experiments are often impossible. Nomothetic laws, the goal of empirical work in the natural sciences, have been very difficult to discover in the social sciences. And analysis, even when successful, may yield a multitude of different ways to look at the same phenomena but no meaningful way to discern which is better.[8]

Corner Cutting

Our second problem paradoxically arises from the fact that data and models have the potential to provide great social benefits. We will discuss these benefits in detail in Chapters 5 and 6. But briefly, data and models provide means of unambiguous communication, the potential to predict the consequences of actions and hence some control over those consequences, at least an appearance of precision and objectivity, and numerical tools that are easily transferable from one person to another. Hence, the information provided by data and models, particularly when it enables prediction and control, has enormous political, economic, and social impact. Unfortunately, however, data and models easily lend themselves to attempts to obtain these benefits without carrying out the rigorous preparations that data and models require, resulting in a "temptation to cut corners." For instance, numerical values easily can be assigned to factors without regard for whether these numbers measure clearly defined or identifiable properties of the factors being studied. But once numbers are assigned, powerful mathematical tools can be used to manipulate them and an aura of precision and rigor can be fostered. Because the use of data and models has become so pervasive in our culture and because mathematical results have a high level of credibility, corner cutting has the potential to inflict significant social harm. We will see several examples as we go along.

Possible Negative Influences of
Scientific Methodology on Culture

The use of data and models may be problematic for deeper reasons than the potential for corner cutting and for misapplying natural science methods. A third problem was raised by Jacques Ellul,[9] William Barrett,[10] and others in their studies of "technique" and its impact on cultures. Informally, we can define technique as a method of thinking that seeks to reduce activities to routines (or "algorithms") that then can be optimized. Thus, the entire process of what Max Weber called the "rationalization of society" is an example of technique. Similarly, computer programs are applications of technique. The efforts of Cornell University home economists in the early part of this century to design kitchens that minimize time and energy used in food preparation are yet another example. Note that scientific research itself is not an example of technique—the application of the scientific method is far from routine! But scientific methodology seeks algorithmic explanations for phenomena; its domain of study is typically aspects of nature that can be described by laws. In fact, practitioners often make the philosophical leap that all of reality can be explained in terms of nomothetic laws.

In the view of its critics, technique has become the predominant thought mode of the late 20th century. One of the primary criticisms of technique that Ellul (1964) makes is that, although it appears neutral, technique is value-laden and the only values it recognizes are efficiency and productivity. That is, the Enlightenment effort to exclude values, norms, and purposes from the search for truth has led to a society in which careful thought about values, norms, and purposes is being neglected. Instead, the implicit values, norms, and purposes of technique (namely, efficiency and productivity) become adopted as societal norms by default and without appropriate consideration of their consequences.

Ellul's (1990) critique is very broad; nevertheless, he cites a number of specific consequences of the growth of technique that relate to the current abundance of human information, our focus here.

■ Western culture has become focused on the rapid, accurate transmission of data not on evaluating its purpose.

■ The nature of information available to us has shifted from "knowledge information" (where to find food, for example) and "organization information" (that which builds cohesive communities, such as stories, music, religious rites) to "service information" (plane schedules, advertising, etc.). Much of the latter does not arise from the natural world at all but is fabricated by people who want us to do things. Hence, much of it is of little value to us.

■ The abundance of human information is modifying personalities in unhealthy ways. It produces mental clutter and confusion (in that we are unable to assimilate all of the information we receive), an inability to verify information for ourselves (there is too much to verify), an inability to correlate and relate events seen in isolation, a weakened capacity to deal with contingency and ambiguity (information received through the media is rarely nuanced), and a detachment from reality. It also fosters an indefiniteness of thought that is unable to define the meaning or nature of new social and cultural objects. (Attribution of meaning requires a framework of principles and values that one can use to evaluate the new object; the development of such a framework is discouraged when technique is regarded as the sole mode of appropriate thinking.)

■ The predominance of technique weakens research into ends and processes—that is, it leads people to dismiss any thinking that is not reducible to formalizable logic.

In summary, this problem deals neither with the potential for abuse of scientific methodology nor with the appropriateness or inappropriateness of its underlying assumptions, as did our previous two problems. Rather, it focuses on some unhappy social consequences of an overly broad adoption of a particular kind of thinking.

Educational Problems

A fourth problem with the use of data and models in the social sciences, it seems to us, is that researchers and practitioners are often trained too narrowly. We have examined a sample of several graduate programs in statistics[11] at major American universities. The programs are very strong in the technical aspects of data analysis. Nevertheless, we were not able to find even one example of a course offered by a graduate-level statistics program that addressed underlying philosophical issues, the history of statistics, or policy implications of statistical analysis. We also examined a number of social science programs. They are understandably broader;

many offer excellent courses in social science philosophy and fundamental methodological problems. But the tendency of such programs is to leave students without a broad perspective on the role of data and models in creating human information. Economics researchers, for example, typically have little training in the dynamics that enter into corporate decision making and the formulation of public policy. Similarly, policy makers may use data with insufficient understanding of its limitations to detect distortions.[12] And few social scientists are encouraged to reflect on the assumptions and values underlying the use of data and models.

The solution of this problem is not simply to replace some of the technical content of statistics and social science programs with content selected from the philosophy and/or history of science. Such an exchange would produce graduates who are technically less prepared. In our experience, we have found that integrating discussion of philosophical and historical material with the technical content of courses can lead to increased *technical* understanding as well as to a broader perspective. This seems to occur because students are better able to grasp the technical material if it is placed in a broader context. Thus, we are convinced that the kind of breadth we are advocating can be achieved without sacrificing technical quality.

▨ THE INFORMATION CYCLE

We have seen that the use of data and models in the social sciences may provide a temptation to (a) misapply methods borrowed from the natural sciences, (b) cut corners by skipping the careful preparation work involved, (c) exclude norms, values, and purposes in the pursuit of nomothetic approaches to the world, and (d) develop excessively narrow educational programs that, in the end, diminish the usefulness of the technical competence they emphasize. To address these problems, we first formulate the notion of the "information cycle," a simple model of the flow of knowledge from the social sciences into cultures. The model is derived from two other types of models: classical models of the scientific method and the software life cycle models used in the field of information systems. Our model is not a standard one in the social sciences. We introduce it here because it has helped us to conceptualize an overview of the role of the social sciences in cultures. We will use it as the framework around which Part II is organized.

The model breaks the process of generating and using information into the following steps:

- Identifying a need for information
- Formulating a precise question
- Selecting a measurement technique
- Collecting data
- Engaging in exploratory data analysis
- Formulating hypotheses, models, or both
- Testing hypotheses
- Promulgating and critiquing results
- Making decisions and/or formulating policy based on results

At many points in this sequence, a need for more information may be identified and the process restarted at the first step. Similarly, after decisions are made and policies formulated, data often are sought to evaluate their effectiveness and to plan for the future. This accounts for the cyclic nature of the process. The steps seem straightforward, but, as we will demonstrate in subsequent chapters, there are many philosophical issues embedded in them. Furthermore, there are many subtle pitfalls that one can fall into while following this seemingly level and well-lit path.

NORMATIVITY

As we have seen, human information has become pervasive in our culture and its use has major social consequences. Earlier in this chapter, we stated this book's central question: "What principles ought to guide the development and use of data and models in the social sciences?" Such principles are often called "norms." Consider a typical definition of the word "norm": "an authoritative rule or standard, a principle of right action, an ideal standard binding on members of a group and serving to guide, control, or regulate proper and acceptable behavior."[13] Other definitions suggest that norms are principles that guide emotion, thought, or both as well as action. For example, the classical goal of normative thought in aesthetics is the development of standards or criteria for evaluating beauty or art. In logic, the classical goal of normative analysis is the development of rules for valid inference. The discipline of logic provides perhaps the clearest example of successful development of norms, as rules of valid inference have been well worked out and command a broad agreement between professional logicians and other scholars. Less agreement on standards has been obtained in aesthetics, but the effort to articulate them continues. In this book, we regard norms as principles capable of guiding the use of data and models so that the potential for harm is minimized and the potential for obtaining benefits is maximized.

To many scientists, the very idea of this book is an oxymoron—in one classical perspective on science, normative considerations are the opposite of empirical and mathematical investigation; introducing norms into the use of data and models would destroy objectivity. Even today, within the economics community, the common perspective is to distinguish "positive" and "normative" analyses—the former being objective and the latter being subjective. Thus, an economist studying the dynamics of inflation would most likely argue that his or her (positive) role is similar to that of a cartographer—he or she tries to draw a map of the portion of the economic landscape surrounding inflation. Norms are what individuals or communities bring to that map as they decide the directions they wish to travel. Thus, (normative) considerations, such as what levels of inflation are acceptable, are left to the political process.

Some philosophers also may be skeptical of an attempt to develop normative principles for the use of data and models in the social sciences. After all, "philosophical attempts to set forth a rational and objective normative ethic have not been notably successful despite the fact that philosophers have been engaged in that activity for the last twenty four centuries."[14] Furthermore, the contemporary focus of ethics has tended either to study metaethics—"a study of the meanings of ethical terms and the methods of justifying ethical statements apart from the actual defense or advocacy of any particular normative claims"[15]—or descriptive ethics— a more or less sociological study of what ethical principles people hold and how they use them. So what we are trying to do here, in articulating particular normative principles, is out of vogue with some philosophers.

But we believe that we have good reasons for proceeding. One reason is that the need for this type of analysis is so great, as we have seen earlier. A second reason is that our question is much smaller than the great ethical questions classical philosophy has sought to answer; in fact, it is small enough that, whereas social scientists may not be able to answer it exhaustively, we believe that they can make significant headway. And third, there is a clear precedent *within science,* namely logic, in which this effort has succeeded. Thus, we will spend the remainder of this chapter explaining how we propose to proceed.

We distinguish two classes of normative principles. The first we call *methodological* or *intrinsic* norms and the second *contextual* or *extrinsic* norms. Methodological norms arise from the capabilities and limitations of the processes of collecting data and developing models. They also include the internal norms characteristic of empirical and mathematical work, such as simplicity, testability, consistency, unbiasedness, elegance, brevity, and fruitfulness. Methodological norms are clearly applicable in research and applications. Consider this metaphor: Imagine a person in a primitive culture who discovers a hammer that some explorer has dropped. By trial and error, that person can discover a lot about the hammer. For instance, it is useful for pounding nails and tent pegs. It's useless for sewing a seam. And it is very effective for disabling one's enemies. Pounding tent pegs is a capability of the hammer; not being able to sew a seam is a limitation. But the question of whether or not it *ought to* be used to disable one's enemies cannot be settled by capabilities and limitations.

Capabilities and limitations can, however, provide methodological norms. Thus, we begin our analysis by introducing a general normative principle— that the methods of gathering and using human information ought to be applied in ways that are consistent with their capabilities and do not exceed their limitations. To apply this principle, one must identify the capabilities and limitations of particular methods and then determine their implications; in fact, most of the normative principles we introduce subsequently will result from applications of this principle. We will assume throughout that the internal norms cited above are being respected.

Neal Koblitz has presented a concrete example of a use of models that violates methodological norms.[16] He says,

> Professor Samuel Huntington [has written] . . . *Political Order in Changing Societies* (1968), in which he suggests various relationships between certain political and sociological concepts: (a) "social mobilization," (b) "economic development," (c) "social frustration," (d) "mobility opportunities," (e) "political participation," (f) "political institutionalization," (g) "political instability." He expresses these relationships in a series of the following equations (p. 55):

$$\text{social mobilization / economic development} =$$
$$\text{social frustration} \; (a/b = c)$$

$$\text{social frustration / mobility opportunities} =$$
$$\text{political participation} \; (c/d = e)$$

$$\text{political participation / political institutionalization} =$$
$$\text{political instability} \; (e/f = g)$$

When he is called upon to summarize his book (e.g., in *Theories of Social Change,* Daniel Bell, Ed.), Huntington emphasizes these equations.

It is doubtful that any of the terms (*a*)-(*g*) can be measured and assigned a numerical value. What are the units of measurement? Will Huntington allow us to operate with these equations using the well-known techniques of ninth-grade algebra? If so, we could infer, for instance, that

$$a = b \times c = b \times d \times e = b \times d \times f \times g$$

i.e., that "social mobilization is equal to economic development times mobility opportunities times political institutionalization times political instability!" (pp. 112-113)

The violation of methodological norms here is that the arithmetic operation of division is defined for numbers but not for the concepts that Huntington employs, and Huntington does not demonstrate how to associate these concepts with numbers. That is, this usage tries to obtain the benefits of precision and clarity that data and models provide without paying the price of respecting their requirements for meaningfulness.

But methodological norms alone are insufficient to provide guidance in important, common decisions that involve the use of human information. As mentioned earlier, the question of when (or if) the hammer should be used to disable an enemy cannot be derived from its capabilities and limitations. This question requires norms not discoverable from the hammer itself. Similarly, problems in engineering and in medical ethics often generate the question "Yes, we can do x, but should we?" Such a question acknowledges that methodological norms alone are insufficient to address the "oughts" in the situation. But it also expresses a confusion about what norms are applicable and even whether the application of norms is appropriate.

In addition to considering methodological norms, it is also necessary to consider *contextual* or *extrinsic* norms. These are the norms that have been called "prima facie duties"[17] and "commonsense norms"—norms, such as honesty, truthfulness, stewardship of natural resources and personal talents, justice, compassion, and respect for other persons. Such norms are applicable when doing research that generates human information as well as in applications that use it; nevertheless, the appropriate application of contextual norms is often subtle.

One test that some philosophers use for an ethical system is whether it generates principles consistent with commonsense norms. We will simply accept these norms and leave justification that these are appropriate norms to philosophers and theologians. Thus, we want to regard all of science but especially the use of data and models in the social sciences (because they are our focus here), as accountable to the ethical standards expressed by the commonsense norms and widely regarded as normative by many cultures.

In the chapters to come, we shall see examples of some uses of data and models that respect and others that violate these norms, although we will focus more heavily on methodological norms. But for clarity we introduce one example at this point.

Robert McNamara was Secretary of Defense under John F. Kennedy and continued in that role under Lyndon Johnson until he resigned in 1968. McNamara successfully implemented many administrative reforms in the Defense Department. He mandated the techniques of planning, budgeting, and evaluating systems. He directed the extensive adoption of systems analysis techniques. And he saved billions of dollars.

McNamara also oversaw the military buildup during the Vietnam War. In a book published in 1995,[18] McNamara acknowledged that he never really believed the war was winnable. McNamara *was* operating out of a set of *methodological* normative principles in his use of formalized methods that were effective in improving efficiency and minimizing costs in the Pentagon. But these principles were inadequate for dealing with the Vietnam War. Perhaps the most obvious commonsense ethical principle is respect for other person's lives. But McNamara was unable to apply this *contextually* normative principle in such a way that it led to effective action to end a war he did not believe was winnable. It seems to us that this is a clear example of the failure to use scientific methodologies with commonsense normative principles.

It is natural at this point to ask whether methodological norms and contextual norms ever conflict. Our answer is this: We do not know, but we have not yet found such an example.

▓ CONCLUSION

Our strategy for the remaining eight chapters is this: First, we establish some context for discussing normative principles for the use of data and models in the social sciences. We will do this by considering the nature of models (and hence some limits built into the modeling process) in Chapter 2 and the intellectual history that has brought us to the abundance of human information we have today in Chapter 3. In subsequent chapters we will look in more detail at the information cycle, although we will not limit ourselves strictly to a discussion of the cycle itself. Chapter 4 will be concerned with values and assumptions implicit in the use of data and models. During this discussion, we will address normative aspects of the first two steps of the information cycle—identification of the need for information and formulation of a precise question. Chapters 5 and 6 will address measurement—that is, selecting a measurement technique and collecting data. Chapter 7 will address data and inference; this discussion will consider the steps of the information cycle dealing with exploratory data analysis and hypothesis formulation and testing. Chapter 8 will address causal and teleological explanations. This topic is closely related to hypothesis testing, decision making, and policy formulation, in that explanations of causes of social phenomena are often sought as a basis for decisions and policy. And last, Chapter 9 will directly address decision making and policy formation.

▓ NOTES

1. ICPSR, p.vii.
2. See Kramer and Conoley (1992).
3. See Murphy et al. (1994).
4. See Tieger and Tieger (1995).
5. February 24, 1995.
6. Two obvious concerns that arise about human information are privacy and security. These questions are extremely important, but because they have been so widely studied and discussed, we will not pursue them here.
7. One of the best pieces of humorous writing in the natural sciences with which we are familiar is a publication called *The Journal of Irreproducible Results*. Several of the most outstanding pieces published in this journal are collected in *The Best of the Journal of Irreproducible Results*. The existence of a humorous publication with such a title certainly dramatizes the importance of reproducibility of results in the natural sciences.
8. Game theory provides a clear example of this phenomenon.

9. Ellul introduced the concept of technique to the English speaking world in 1964 with the translation of his book *La Technique ou l'enjeu du Siecle*. The English title is *The Technological Society*. Both French and German contain distinct words to refer to technology as artifact and technology as a way of thinking. Ellul's French title refers to the latter. Because English did not contain such a distinction at the time, the translator rendered the title using the word "technological" but then used the English word "technique" throughout the book. Subsequent works by Ellul, *The Technological System* (1980) and *The Technological Bluff* (1990), have explored these notions further. The critique summarized here is found in the latter.

10. See Barrett (1978).

11. Carnegie-Mellon University, Florida State University, Michigan State University, Princeton University, Stanford University, University of California at Berkeley, University of Chicago, University of Michigan, University of Rochester, and Yale University.

12. Nevertheless, there is an organization in Washington, D.C. called STATS that seeks to inform and educate journalists on common distortions.

13. Based on the Oxford *Unabridged dictionary*.

14. See Neilsen (1967, p. 119).

15. This description is from personal correspondence with Dr. John Edelman of the Philosophy Department, Nazareth College, Rochester, NY, 14610. But there are many published references that define metaethics. For instance, see Frankena (1973, pp. 4-5).

16. Koblitz (1981).

17. See McCloskey (1969).

18. See McNamara (1995).

CHAPTER

TWO

Modeling

Chapter 1 introduced one aspect of the nature of our age. In contrast to earlier times, ours is known not as the era of faith nor reason nor ideology but of information—of rapid, inexpensive, widely dispersed access to an incredible volume of information. Chapter 1 also introduced the topic of this book: An age of information requires wisdom and discernment in knowing what information is to be created for which issues, how to select from the information available, how to organize, analyze, draw inferences from and present this information appropriately, how to inform policy from it, and what normative principles to apply in these endeavors. This chapter and the next provide some intellectual and historical context for examining the limits of the use of data and models in social science.

Modeling is a first step in moving toward analysis and policy, a crucial step that determines the usefulness of the work that follows. Modeling is the process of *formalizing* our framework for interpreting the world around us by *abstracting* from a reality that is otherwise too complex to understand. In fact, modeling is the central intellectual method that characterizes most empirical and mathematical approaches to social science.

Why start our discussion with a chapter on modeling? The theory of science that has dominated the social sciences until recently, the so-called "received view"[1] associated with positivism, would instead generally place

23

observation and measurement prior to modeling. One account of modeling[2] more consistent with this received view introduces our subject in this way:

> An examination of the origins of any scientific field, be it astronomy or anatomy, physics or psychology, indicates that the discipline began with a mass of observations and experiments. It is natural, then, that the first steps in quantifying the subject should involve the collection, presentation and treatment of data. . . . Once enough data have been collected and adequately analyzed, the researcher tries to imagine a process which accounts for these results. It is this activity, the mental or pencil-and-paper creation of a theoretical system that is the topic of this book. In the scientific literature this activity is commonly known as theory construction and analysis. We shall refer to it as the construction, development, and study of mathematical models. (p. 1)

We believe that this account reverses the proper order of things, though a full discussion of the matter must wait until Chapters 3 and 4. Whereas observation and theory construction should develop with much interplay, theories tend to guide our selection of relevant observations. Hence, we need to begin our work with a consideration of what it means to form a theory—that is, to model a situation.

We therefore begin with this chapter on the nature of modeling, followed by a chapter that draws lessons from past attempts to understand the world through the use of data and models.

GAINING UNDERSTANDING BY LOSING INFORMATION

> Model: A formal or informal framework of analysis which seeks to abstract from the complexities of the real world those characteristics . . . that are crucial for an understanding of the behavioral, institutional and technical relationships [that] underlie [the real world]. The intention is to facilitate the explanation of . . . phenomena, and . . . the generation of . . . forecasts.[3] (p. 277)

Modeling is, first, an attempt at helpful simplification. In the real world there are many billions of events, facts, relationships, and actions. If we are to get anywhere in understanding something, we must have a model or conceptual framework that guides us in picking out the information that is relevant to the issue before us. Facts alone do not give us understanding about why something has happened, how something operates, what is responsible for change, or what is likely to cause changes in the future. We are forced to abstract from a complicated reality to understand it, and a good model condenses the confusion of the world into a form that is both comprehensible and helpful. We always comprehend the world by mental structures that affect our perception, and models are skeletal rough approximations of the part of the world we are out to analyze. Modeling is the development of analogies and metaphors, likening reality to mental constructions that are focused in particular (and we hope precise) ways. Modeling involves us in identifying which things in the world are problems and what their potential causes and solutions are.

As a simple example, consider the way in which economists and lay economic observers use such phrases as "market economy" or "the retail market for shoes." There is not a literal market for shoes—no auctioneer calling out prices to vendors and potential buyers, no simultaneous striking of many bargains, not even a central place at which most of the purchases of shoes take place. The same can be said for many of the transactions that take place in a so-called market economy. Yet "the market" is thought of as a useful model of how some economies function, a metaphor that may guide one in picking out some important features and results of an economic system. From the incredible variety among purchase sites, seller personalities, buyer sophistication, and design options, the metaphor of a market guides one in abstracting salient features of the economic process: By thinking *as if* there were large auctions in a market economy, our attention is focused in a particular direction (e.g., toward incomes, population size, production costs) for considering the determinants of economic outcomes and simultaneously focused away from other potential influences (e.g., class, personal motives, gender).

A crucial part of the modeling process is developing and testing the most *helpful* abstractions, those that leave out the unimportant to make the important more obvious. One useful study of our modern situation emphasizes this point by beginning with these words.[4]

> In many countries of the world today, mathematical modeling is a major force in decision making for both the public and the private sectors. Policies with wide-ranging and far-reaching effects for millions of people may be based on projections derived from computer analyses of data. . . . This growth in the numbers, complexity, and significance of models raises many

ethical questions such as: What is the proper relationship between the model builder and the model user? Should model builders assume professional responsibility for the results of their models? Do model builders have a responsibility to those affected by the results of their models besides their clients? (p. 1)

One must develop skill in noticing the things about a particular situation that make one model useful but a different model harmful, and dexterity in abandoning a model when the situation changes sufficiently to make the model inappropriate.

So, modeling is an attempt at helpful simplification of reality. It also frequently has become an attempt at mathematization of situations. Part of the motive of mathematics, as with modeling in general, is to make the world more intelligible through the use of mental structures, symbols, and abstractions. So, it makes sense that mathematics may be necessary to get at some points of modeling in the social and decision sciences.

The process of modeling a situation mathematically can itself be modeled as a series of steps. Before we explore them in detail, we summarize a study that relies on modeling to explore an important problem. It will serve as an example for several of the ideas that follow.

AN EXAMPLE:
MAJOR LEAGUE DISCRIMINATION

How did racial discrimination affect the fortunes of U.S. major league baseball teams in the 1950s, the early years of integration? Was bigotry expensive and in that sense self-defeating? Or was integration financially costly, an uphill battle against market forces?

A widely read journal article[5] approached the question using some common economic reasoning: Proven black players were available from the Negro Leagues for a fraction of the cost of developing less-talented white players; teams that ignore this source of value should experience both higher franchise costs and worse team performance. Thus, integrated teams should have an economic advantage over teams that discriminate, unless fans' bigotry results in lower attendance for integrated teams.

The authors tested these propositions with data from major league teams between 1950 and 1959. To see if the inclusion of black players increased team performance, the number of games won in each year was regressed on either the number of black players on the team that year or (as a check on the trustworthiness of the previous result) the cumulative number of black-player-years the team had employed by the year in question. To control for team quality before the inclusion of black players, the regression included the percentage of games won between 1946 and 1949, when very few black players were on major league teams. The authors concluded that, "for the . . . 1950-1959 period, each additional black player is estimated to have meant two additional wins per year."[6]

To explore whether fans boycotted integrated teams, the authors reasoned that attendance would normally be influenced by a team's won/lost record but also would be influenced by the presence and number of black players if race-based boycotts existed. In the study, annual attendance for each team in each year was regressed on the number of black players on each team in each year, number of games won that year, and average attendance for the team in the 1946 to 1949 period (to standardize for teams' historic attendance patterns before racial integration). A positive coefficient on the black-player variable indicated that there was indeed an economic incentive to integrate, which the authors estimated to be greater than $55,000 per year per black player.

THE MODELING PROCESS

We have said that the process of modeling a situation mathematically can itself be modeled as a series of steps. It is time to explore them.

1. First, one formulates the problem informally. Although we consider problem formulation at some length in Chapter 3, we can say here that the initial genesis of a model is a notoriously foggy issue.[7]

> The formulation phase has traditionally been a murky and understudied aspect of the modeling process. It is here that the modeler works from a "sense" of the problem to assemble the elements and relationships that will make certain simplifying assumptions and to address questions, such as which factors to include and which to ignore in the model. The formulation stage is crucial because it is both difficult and important to decide whether one formulation is better than another, particularly because the implications of a given form of problem abstraction are difficult to discern so early in the process. (p. 2)

In our baseball discrimination example, much of the genesis of the model seems to come by habit: Professionals trained in a particular discipline (in this case, economics) fall into patterns when setting up a model.

2. One's approach to a problem should be stated as precisely as possible, carefully defining as many phrases involved as possible. (We will have more to say about definitions in Chapter 6.) This step is sometimes called "construction of the real model," because we are still considering "real" things rather than symbols that represent real things. This continues the process of abstraction, because one usually must approximate or typify the situation to even describe it. We also cannot define everything, so we are immediately forced to identify the patterns and choose the topics and items that are central to the issue at hand. Some other items will not be defined because they are less central, and still others, so-called "primitive notions," will be left undefined because they are so essential to the problem that they only could be defined in terms of themselves.

In our baseball example several simplifications come early in the model: the period of study is limited to one decade; performance of the franchise is measured simply by number of games won; all changes in team performance are attributed to the influence of black players; individual differences among black players are ignored.

3. The modeler begins to abstract from the real model a description of the processes that are taking place and express these in mathematical symbols. This translates the real model into a mathematical model, a set of constructed symbols and operations that represent real items and operations. This is a crucial step, with several characteristic features.

- It is a creative, nonmechanical operation.

- It is therefore true that the same real model may be represented by several different mathematical models. One mathematical model may function better than others in representing certain features of the real model. (And remember that even the real model may not capture the essential features of the actual situation under study—the mathematical model puts us at least two steps distant from "the real world.") For example, the baseball article authors had to choose a type of equation (linear, nonlinear, with or without interactions among the variables, etc.) before preceding with their regressions.

■ It is therefore likely that there is no single best model of any particular situation, none that will more accurately reflect and predict reality than all others. Reality is too complex and models too limited. It is more likely that several models each shed light on different facets of the real situation. Choice of the "right" model depends in part on the motives of the investigator: the questions being asked, the outcomes that are valued or dismissed, or even the habits of mind that the investigator has never questioned.

■ This implies that a particular *mathematical* model of a situation may be rejected or accepted on grounds that are not particularly objective, such as the modeler's judgment about which issues or outcomes are most important.

■ Rejection of a particular mathematical model does not necessarily bring into question the value of the underlying real model. We explore this further in Chapter 3.

■ Therefore, we suggest a first norm intrinsic to the modeling process: Decision makers who rely on models should employ several different ways of modeling and exploring the situation over which they have authority. Thus, for instance, human resource managers must be careful not to become locked into a single formal evaluation process for employees, because it is likely to be effective only for some few parts of the employee's responsibilities. Researchers should likewise be wary of the hegemony of any single methodological approach. Empirical researchers should approach a given situation in several ways before claiming that anything has been demonstrated or proven. In fact, one hallmark of the information age should be that persons who work with models should develop the discipline to deliberately set aside their favorite or familiar models when approaching problems, to explore the situation from other angles.

4. The mathematical model must be studied and manipulated, with an eye toward exposing implications and forecasts for the underlying real model—that is, to create new information. In the discrimination article, we are given performance and financial estimates of the effects of integration. If the mathematics becomes unsolvable, simulation of the situation by computer may be possible, though this involves yet another layer of abstraction away from the real system.

5. The analyst compares these theoretical results and predictions to the behavior of the real system and revisits each part of the exercise if the theory does not perform well.

KINDS OF MODELS

Before considering the strengths and weaknesses of this approach to a study of the real world, we should indicate that there are several different classes of models. We will briefly explore why each type is appropriate in different situations and subject to different tests of validity, first by discussing how each treats data, then by considering how each approaches reality.

Consider the three ways in which a model can treat data: *Stochastic* models incorporate data that are particular observations of a random variable,[8] whereas *deterministic* models claim a precise knowledge about the data involved. (The normal curve is an example of a stochastic model and has seen wide application in all manners of decision making. The baseball discrimination article relies on regression analysis, another type of stochastic model. Most linear programming models are deterministic models that return a particular set of numbers for a solution.) Not all models rely on data collection for their application; they are by nature *nonempirical,* such as some forms of game theory or Banzhaf's power index (which will be discussed in Chapter 4). These are not data-driven nor looking to data for generalizations. They do not originate directly from observations, nor are they expressed statistically. They are, instead, general principles deduced from an idealized description of something, and as such it is sometimes impossible to test these models' ultimate validity.

Recall that our final step in constructing a mathematical model was to compare the model's theoretical results and predictions to the behavior of the real system, revisiting each part of the modeling exercise if the theory does not perform well. For models that are *stochastic* (i.e., that treat each bit of data as an event drawn from a larger pool of likely possible outcomes), there is a well-developed body of thought in the discipline of statistics that serves in these comparisons of theory with reality. For example, one might use an ANOVA (analysis of variance) table or a chi-square test to evaluate a theory concerning which salespersons' traits are associated with larger commissions or which school characteristics are related to different types of student achievement. These are stochastic models; even if the model proves to be defensible, we cannot exactly predict students' achievement by merely measuring a school's characteristics carefully. There still will be some unexplained, stochastic variation in student achievement, so a model is not necessarily rejected if it does not predict perfectly. Hence, we need statistical tests to decide how imperfect a model can become before being rejected.

For *deterministic* models, knowledge of enough initial conditions gives one confidence about the entire future of the system. Compared to stochastic models, it is easier to test these models' results directly, by comparing model predictions to actual events.[9] But matters become more complicated when deterministic models are used as simplified approximations of stochastic real systems. This practice would seem to give the deterministic model a verification ace-in-the-hole: If the model's predictions deviate from real-world events, the error always can be attributed to the simplification.

This complication arises routinely when spreadsheet analysis (usually a deterministic model) is used to analyze and predict a stochastic situation (like government budgets or school enrollments). It also can arise because of other, seemingly unrelated, mistakes. Say, for example, that a school administrator misapplies some statistical tests in a stochastic study of student achievement. He (incorrectly) believes he has identified the three school characteristics that most benefit students—computer classrooms, special reading programs, and high teacher salaries. He presents these findings to the school board as a deterministic model that approximates the original stochastic model, with such phrases as "given a cutting-edge computer classroom, we can improve student SAT scores by 5%." The board accepts his argument and funds the three characteristics that were advocated. If student test scores remain flat, it may be attributed to random, stochastic movements of the test scores. Because "we know" that the three characteristics affect achievement, analysts may search for other characteristics that have changed (causing the flattening of test scores) rather than revisit the original study of student achievement.

Because *nonempirical* models are difficult to test directly, they are often defended on the basis of the helpfulness of the implications derived from them. They may be intrinsically untestable. For example, Banzhaf's index of political power is more a definition of power than a model of an empirical phenomenon.

Rather than classify models according to the ways they treat data, we could classify them by three ways in which they approach reality. *Deductive* models often explicitly incorporate some directive guidelines about what ought to be done in a particular situation. For instance, linear programming models include an explicit factor that is to be maximized or minimized, such as profit or cost. A director of a third-world demonstration farm might use a deductive linear programming model as a guide to mix animal feed using local ingredients so that the nutritional needs of the animals are met at minimum cost. She could use the same kind of model to calculate a feed mix that maximizes independence of the community from imports while still feeding the animals well.

These deductive models are sometimes more highly idealized or abstracted than *inductive* models, which aim to describe some facet of reality as it actually is. The biggest class of inductive models is the stochastic or statistical analysis class, such as normal curves. The school administrator who studies the reasons for student achievement and the authors of the baseball discrimination study are engaged in inductive modeling, trying to describe how some part of reality works.

Computer advances also have allowed development of *knowledge representation,* models that seek to represent human judgment and experience by incorporating the thinking processes of humans.[10]

THE POWER OF
FORMAL MODELING

It is no accident that formal modeling has become a primary tool-of-the-trade in the management, policy, social, and decision sciences. Used properly in the right situation, the benefits of good theory and formal modeling can be very impressive.

For example, think of the achievements of the U.S. space program in the 1960s. We should consider that the impressive scientific advances of that era took place within a larger context. They may not have flowered nor come together into a successful venture without being surrounded by an administrative culture of deliberate, careful formal modeling. The process of coordinating millions of workers' hours with hundreds of thousands of tasks to deliver the Apollo moon landing within 10 years, with a limited budget, would have been impossible for informal, seat-of-the-pants administrators; it required the judicious use of formal modeling.

Deductive modeling allowed the many interdependent tasks to be ordered with a minimum of wasted time; inductive modeling considered failure rates of various components and directed the pursuit of backup systems; deterministic models directed the composition of astronaut menus.

As the decades have passed, careful formal modeling has become common for more and more of modern industry, services, and public policy. Building and marketing new cars, presenting expert legal testimony, maintaining a solvent Social Security system, conducting medical research, and evaluating the effects of welfare reform proposals are a few cases in which the use of formal modeling is now considered commonplace and essential.

What is the source of the power of formal modeling? Consider two classes of reasons.

1. Modeling can expose similarities in the form of problems that previously appeared to be unrelated, clarify thinking by requiring that familiar concepts be stated in precise language so that mathematical symbols can be used to keep the logic tidy, allow simulations of otherwise costly projects, and even promote some forms of social justice. In these senses formal modeling has what we might call an "instrumental" benefit: it is a helpful instrument for pursuing the goal of forming theories, but the modeling remains external to the actual development of theory. Theory formation is important because theories are our generalizations about cause and effect, our guides in understanding how reality operates; adding formal modeling to a theory may have an instrumental benefit, much like adding a gasoline supplement to your car. It makes the machine work more smoothly but does not alter its basic form. No doubt this is the image of formal modeling that animates most of its users.

2. The introduction of formalism usually is also more organically connected to theory. The presence of formalism can be like the addition of a new design engineer, looking over the shoulder of the mechanic who is constructing a new engine. Formalism then affects not only the smooth operation of theories but, for better or worse, influences the development of theories from the very beginning. A person approaching baseball discrimination with an interest in estimating regression equations about it will clearly be drawn toward different emphases than a sports journalist approaching the same topics.

We can consider several potential benefits of modeling that are directly related to this organic link between formalized modeling and the development of theories.

1. Formal modeling can force one to *have* some theory and to make a statement of it. Near the start of this chapter we argued that in a complex world everyone will have some set of abstractions, whether acknowledged or otherwise. But formalism sometimes encourages one to be precise, efficient, and logical in stating one's theory and assumptions. Informal modeling can be haphazard, uninformed by any particular coherent theory and not easily tested or made to answer to counterfactual circumstances.[11] Of course, informal or prose statements of theory sometimes do help loose thinking to become rigorous and well organized, but formalism may create more pressure for rigor and a defensible framework by encouraging one to be explicit about how one is abstracting from the world.

2. Formal modeling sometimes causes the discovery of theoretical concepts that would have otherwise remained veiled or incomprehensible but prove to be quite common and useful once we are aware of them. The importance of marginal analysis (marginal cost, marginal revenues), a commonplace topic in areas ranging from antitrust cases and regulatory hearings to environmental policy and lost earnings lawsuits, was established largely by formal modeling.

This process of discovery is not limited to the creation of more knowledge. By showing which assumptions are necessary to a particular result, discovery can sometimes be the ironic sort that demonstrates the limits of our knowledge. For example, some[12] have instinctively felt that international trade will drive all nations' "factor prices" (wages, profit rates, land rentals) to similar levels and have therefore (especially in wealthy countries) opposed international trade. But the long list of unlikely assumptions required by the factor-price equalization theorem (provided by Paul Samuelson in the late 1940s), along with the failure of trade to equalize factor prices, have convinced many[13] that fears (or hopes) of common worldwide wage rates are unfounded.

3. Mathematical modeling allows some *derivations* that simply would not be possible otherwise. It is the only way to solve some problems. An inventory manager, who hourly must solve a set of simultaneous equations to keep her suppliers and clients happy, would be in a difficult position if

prose were her only tool. But with a good model and a computer she can solve the equations almost effortlessly.

THE LIMITATIONS OF FORMAL MODELING

We have catalogued the potential benefits of formal modeling for solving problems and developing theories. Some cautions are also called for. Despite its promise, formalism has become an easy target of dissatisfaction. The effortless ease with which our inventory manager solves equations may lull her into reliance on the model when it does not fit; precise, rigorous statements of assumptions can force intuitive, qualitative considerations to disappear from view. For instance, those who have lived with the aftermath of a modeling-approach-gone-haywire can attest that the preceding strengths of formal modeling represent only one face of a two-edged blade. Each beneficial use of its power we have listed is balanced by a negative potential.

1. Because formal modeling forces one to state theory in a precise, logical, and efficient manner, it creates a danger that only the *mathematical* assumptions will be stated, and the more formidable behavioral assumptions in the model will lay buried, implicit, and perhaps unreasonable. For example, economists are prone to carefully state assumptions of linearity, homogeneity, homotheticity, and other mathematical properties, while remaining silent on the implicit assumptions of "economic man" rationality, inexpensive technological change, and universal social mobility. Some would argue that entire subdisciplines within economics, psychology, sociology, or management science are built on unreal abstractions of persons' actual materialism, sexual drives, class background, or machine-like capabilities, all hidden in the formal modeling.

2. Modeling may bias not only our statement of assumptions but also our choice of questions or variables to be explored. In this way the power of mathematical modeling in clarifying obscure topics is offset by its ability to simultaneously cloak other meaning.

Among the things of interest that are difficult to formalize, qualitative variables are especially susceptible to becoming theoretical orphans when we move from real to mathematical models, not because they are unimportant but because they are not given to easy measurement and symbolic manipulation.[14] For example, mathematical workplace evaluation models that emphasize easily measurable quantities (such as sales revenues, timeliness, or attendance at formal training) can silence qualitative issues (like credibility, leadership, or contribution to team spirit) that are crucial to good decision making.

But it is not only qualitative variables that are susceptible to loss. The kinds of questions a professional asks are always to some extent set by the context of her or his profession. When formal modeling becomes the context for an entire profession, one may begin to stop asking some important questions and start asking the wrong questions. In economics, for example, the presumed context is often "equilibrium" or "maximization." Such assumptions commit one to a certain set of questions and close off consideration of large tracts of reality. The last decade of work in chaos theory and dynamic nonlinear systems indicates that the commitment to equilibrium modeling has led the profession to dismiss as "random noise" some data that should have been of interest.

Said differently, models necessarily simplify. But in some situations, especially those involving humans, the most essential feature of a situation may be its very complexity. Thus, modeling inherently misrepresents. The values of the mathematician—precision and elegance—replace useful correspondence to reality as the most significant features of the model.

For example, models of groups (or of any aggregate) typically erase individuality. In a community, each person understands other people and situations differently. But modeling seeks a unitary, transferable formulation of a situation. Thus, it inherently loses the quality of multiplicity of perspectives. Models of individuals typically focus on particular features, thus losing the person, because persons are found in their totality.

Because human uniqueness is often omitted in models, they easily may omit essential ethical considerations that grow out of our treatment of individual persons. They easily lend themselves to using persons as means to an end.

Thus, models are inherently incapable of capturing some central features of our humanness. This feature differentiates the social sciences' use of models from that of the natural sciences.

3. The desire for generality can cause one's method to be overplayed, such that the modeling tail wags the substantive dog. We may be presented with elegant but hollow theoretical constructs that have less to do with

real-world policy than was hoped. Formalism promises clarity but sometimes delivers it by making strange assumptions, pretending to solve a problem when it has not.

We already have mentioned a few considerations about the baseball discrimination paper that might fall into this category. All changes in team performance after 1950 are attributed to changes in the number of black players, and attendance by those not bigoted is taken to depend only on won-loss record and pre-1950 attendance. But ask a larger question: Does the study tell us why integration began to happen in the 1950s? No. It might tell us that there was a financial incentive to integrate in the 1950s, but this is a limited result. If markets routinely create financial incentives to integrate, as the original reasoning in the modeling exercise indicated, why didn't integration happen much earlier? Was there no similar incentive in, say, the 1940s? If not, why not? Why does integration appear to be still relatively rare in the leadership structures of professional sports, where fan prejudices would seem to be much less influential?

4. Though formalism can allow derivations that are otherwise impossible, this power often seems to cause the initial simplifying assumptions to be quickly forgotten. As we explore in Chapters 4 and 6, this power also seems to encourage professions toward attempts to be precise about things that are inherently vague or not yet sufficiently understood.

One might say that these difficulties are not *due to* formal mathematical modeling, at least not directly. Humans always impose structure through abstraction, and the modeling may be merely a way of forming this structure solidly. In fact, every means of abstracting, formal or otherwise, is prone to some form of the four weaknesses we have listed. So we do *not* claim that the social, management, and policy realms never can be helped by formalism.

Yet one always brings an angle of vision that influences choices of methods and assumptions. Beyond the limitations of the mathematical modeling "tools" that have been listed, we must also acknowledge the particular angle of vision that develops around their use. We might call this angle of vision *the culture of formalism*. This culture of formalism encourages particular patterns for asking questions, making assumptions, and using techniques, even when these are inappropriate. These patterns institutionalize the limitations of formal modeling and dull our senses to the topics that cannot be approached through formal methods. For example, formal modeling made the success of the U.S. space program possible, but it also produced an internal NASA culture that was being criticized by the 1980s for its resistance to necessary change.

One feature of the information age is the dissemination of this culture of formalism more widely throughout the general populace. This raises several new difficulties for formal modeling.

5. We face an explosion of user-friendly modeling software and with it can come pressure to justify formally more everyday decisions. This may accelerate the use of formal models for sophisticated purposes by relatively untrained operators who may not understand the intricacies, assumptions, values, or limits of the models.[15]

■ Models designed for routine situations are likely to be applied in exceptional situations for which they were not designed and in which they do not function well. This happens because of the lack of expertise on the part of users and pressure to "rationalize" practices into standard policies that are applied uniformly. As the culture of formalism expands, the potential for damage due to this problem multiplies.

■ We may generalize these concerns. As many operators make more decisions about more important issues, society faces an increased risk of what has been called Type III error—the use of a good model for the wrong situation. In the process the wrong decision is made, though (in fact, because) the procedures of the modeling exercise were followed perfectly. For instance, loan officers may have difficulty approving worthwhile projects that are atypical; a hiring or promotion decision that formerly had considered qualitative issues may be reduced to a comparison of test scores; formalized stock-trading programs may sometimes affect stock prices in counterproductive ways.

■ Operator ineptness and pressures to rationalize processes encourage the "typing" of persons. For instance, standardized testing (such as an IQ test) is sometimes used to sort people into an "ability" hierarchy. We consider this example in detail in Chapter 6.

6. One might say that the problems in #5 are not difficult to solve: Just train more experts in the intricacies of modeling. This is no doubt part of a good response to the situation, though there remain several problems. The culture of formalism seems by nature to mitigate against the kind of broad, well-informed education that is necessary for making one a good

modeler: A competent modeler must actually know a great deal about the world, and know it from many different angles, if he or she is to have the wisdom and dexterity to appreciate when and where a particular model "fits."

7. Because of the potential benefits of good modeling, those who are gifted modelers earn relatively good salaries for their expertise. Clients who have money will be able to afford them. What of the other potential clients who face problems and decisions that are just as pressing and difficult, but who cannot afford good advice? As they become more distanced from the world of gifted modelers, clients who could benefit from modeling may become less aware of the potential benefits of good modeling. Intellectual capital is thus subtly concentrated around those with financial capital. These always have been serious issues, but we judge that they will become more compelling and problematic as the information age matures.

SOME FIRST GUIDELINES

We have argued that formal modeling, as nearly everything else, is a good thing that can be terribly misused. It is also rapidly becoming a part of the basic fabric of contemporary culture, not only in the social sciences but in public and private enterprise decision making. If modeling has limits and potential abuses, how might we know when we have gone too far, recognize difficulties in others' work, and plan ahead to avoid the pitfalls as much as possible? It is time to draw together our discussion into some normative guidelines. They may seem to be only a wish list at this point, but throughout the rest of the book we aim to develop some strategies for implementing them.

1. Those who are not professional modelers should remain aware that alternate models for a situation will lead to different results and policies. The results may even be contradictory, though they all will have a "scientific" appearance. Various models usually expose only some facets of a situation and even then only apply under the specific conditions assumed in the model.

2. Users, therefore, need to remain open to several different ways to model and explore a situation, rather than becoming locked-in to a specific approach; they should especially beware of applying a model of routine activity to exceptional circumstances and of "typing" persons through modeling.

Point #1 also raises the possibility that a model will be unethically bent toward the desired results or that modeling might only become a tool of persuasion and self-expression rather than a means to explore reality. We propose several disciplines.

3. Users need to deliberately create openness for the evaluation of models that are employed in the workplace or professions. This might, first, involve developing a set of questions[16] to be asked of model builders. The questions should sort out the assumptions, limits, and values implicit in the model; explore which aspects of the model are transferable to reality, what features of reality the model exposes, and what features of reality are better studied by a different model; and expose the things that are left out of the model, including qualitative variables and directions of questioning that are cut off by the model.

4. Modeler and model user must maintain very open communication during development of the model. The modeler must be questioned to be sure the data are understood, the assumptions and values of the user are being represented, the effects of the model's assumptions on its results are clear, and the model and actions based on it have the desired effect.

5. Part of the discipline of modeling should involve peer review and open debate. Modelers need to be scrupulous about making explicit the assumptions and limits of their work. Model builders should, as much as possible, make their data and methodology public so that replication and repeated specification can take place. Part of this review should be done by those who are affected by the results of the model but are neither the modeler nor the model user.

6. The modeling professions should aim to internalize within each piece of work the process of exploring how robust are the results. The fields of social and decision sciences are at some disadvantage in replication and repeated specification relative to the natural sciences, because studies outside of disciplines using controlled experiments are often less directly cumulative than natural sciences can be; social science studies often go beside each other, rather than being presented serially, so that testing the fragility of assumptions is left to unconnected later articles that look for problems in the initial model. Modeling practitioners in nonexperimental fields therefore must develop the discipline of studying a situation with several different models and reporting all of the results, exploring how robust are the results of each model.

7. The last paragraph explores only one of a series of potential changes in the education of modelers. Professional modelers need the communication skills necessary to converse with clients in the ways we have suggested in paragraphs #3 and #4 above. Their education needs to be wide and liberal so that they can know the modeled situation from several points of view. They should consider their responsibility for the success or failure of a model and consider how to value those who are neither modelers nor model users but are still affected by the model. They need to develop the discipline of constantly asking which aspects of the model are transferable to reality and which are not.

Besides the behavior of modelers and model users, there are some cultural effects of the explosion of modeling that should be considered.

8. The educational system for modelers must keep up with the explosion in the construction and use of models, as computers become faster and omnipresent. As we have suggested and discuss from a different angle in Chapter 7, the wise use of models requires a strong general education, as well as some specific training in the benefits and limits of modeling.

9. To the extent that modeling is powerful and useful, there is some danger that groups who cannot afford good modelers will find themselves at an increasing disadvantage. At the very least, professional modelers should consider how their work may inadvertently entrench advantaged and disadvantaged groups.

10. There is some danger that, because models appear to be "precise," they will be taken too seriously. Models attempt to separate the most important from the less important, but often in the social and decision sciences any one question is embedded in "the whole system." This makes it harder to model, experiment, and measure; things change quickly, and often simultaneously, so that we are not always sure if the constants in a model have been constant. Model theorems in these fields are therefore fuzzy, with approximate results, and a result can be demonstrable without being reasonable. These themes figure prominently in Chapters 7 and 8, where we consider the role of statistics and claims about causation in social sciences.

11. Social and decision sciences must live with soft data and few controlled experiments. It is therefore difficult to draw a hard inference. The more abstraction and the less experimental data in a situation, the

longer the chain of reasoning becomes, and the more subject to fads the results become.

12. Points #9 and #10 imply that we might help the general culture avoid faddish influence from overrated formal models by taking a careful look at measurement and inference in the social sciences. We explore these topics in Chapters 5 through 7.

▨ NOTES

1. The phrase is due to Putnam (1962).
2. Maki and Thompson (1973).
3. The MIT *Dictionary of modern economics* (1986).
4. Wallace (1994).
5. See Gwartney and Haworth (1974).
6. Gwartney and Haworth (1974, p. 877).
7. Wallace (1994).
8. A random variable is a numerical variable that takes on various values with some probability other than one; the value cannot be determined or fully predicted before observation. See, for example, Kmenta (1971, p. 5).
9. To reject a deterministic model is rarely straightforward, though, because even deterministic models often will contain coefficients that must be estimated from the real world by using statistical methods.
10. A third way to classify models is by their form. For example, models can be symbolic, procedural, relational, or rule-based. See, for example, Wallace (1994, p. 2).
11. For example, economic reforms in parts of Eastern Europe in the late 1980s and early 1990s were followed by economic downturns. Did reform cause the downturn? By the mid-1990s several countries elected new governments whose answer was "yes." But this model has not answered the "counterfactual" questions, questions about conditions that did not occur but were possible: How bad a downturn would have occurred in the early 1990s if the reforms had *not* been made? Only a formal model can explore such a question. It is likely that the economies, already in steep decline in the 1980s, would have crashed even deeper without the reform process than they did with it. Thus one test of a good model is its ability to consider counterfactual, "what if" questions.
12. Notable recent advocates in the United States might include Patrick Buchanan and Ross Perot.
13. See, for example, Lindert (1991, p. 78): "The theorem is more than just remarkable. It is also wrong. Even the most casual glance at the real world shows that the predictions of the factor-price equalization theorem are not borne out."
14. Maki and Thompson (1973, p. 4).
15. For a consideration of several of these issues, see, for example, Wallace (1994).
16. See, for example, Wallace (1994).

Dreams and Disappointments

▓ THE LONG CONVERSATION

Every nation or human community that hopes to survive and prosper must find a way to make peace in the face of deeply held personal differences. Values and beliefs are rarely identical within large communities, and a brief survey of recent history is enough to force sober reflection on the person who thinks that these differences are trivial.

The social science community is one of these human communities that must come to terms with differences in values and beliefs among its members. We have seen that this community is at the core of the enormous volume of human information that characterizes our time. This community, therefore, has great influence on shaping modern culture, from the most public issues like welfare reform and foreign policy to more intimate topics like family planning and college admission. It is now time to begin facing some difficult questions about this social science community: Do the values and beliefs of social scientists influence their work? If so, is there still hope of developing social sciences that transcend personal differences and are

43

"true for everybody?" Or is the hope of making wise group choices via carefully ordered knowledge a vain hope, swamped by the stubborn individuality of personal differences?

One way of dealing with differences is to assume them away. It was once assumed that values and beliefs only mattered outside of the sciences, even the social sciences. Except for a few core values—clear reasoning, accuracy and truthfulness in recording data, and rapid public dissemination of results—science was considered the world of fact, and the scientist's other values were not to influence the science. This tight distinction between facts and values was thought to hold promise as one way of building culture independent of questions of value. But this view of science has been seriously questioned, especially during the last 50 years.

In this chapter we want to give an introduction to the professional conversation about just what kinds of valuing are required in the social sciences. This background is central to the concerns of this book. In this volume we are trying to articulate norms for data and models in the social sciences. This will involve trying to make room within the social sciences for the consideration of values and beliefs, without making the social sciences relativistic or inconsequential. This chapter, therefore, is part of a much broader contemporary discussion of the proper place of values and beliefs within the academic disciplines, the effects of the enlightenment on culture, and the future of academic life. This is a robust and important discussion; one author has written of it as a battle for the soul of the university.[1] We cannot hope to consider here all of the vast literature on these topics or even on the narrower topic of different perspectives on science, but we will introduce some issues our disciplines must consider in this discussion by giving a broad historical context for the conversation about values, data, and models in the social sciences. We then go on to examine the information cycle, step-by-step, in the following chapters.

There are several spots from which we might trace the history of the high hopes held for data, models, and formal mathematical reasoning. The Greek attempts to systematize logic and axiomatize geometry, an axiomatization that endured for over 2,000 years, would be a good starting point. Developments of the middle ages, including the principle of Occam's razor that informs so much of modeling, would be another. But our chief interest is in providing a context for the uses of data and models in the modern social and decision sciences. Thus, our emphasis will be on the modern era, beginning with Descartes.

▓ DREAMS FOR DATA AND MODELS

The vision of using modeling, empirical observation, and mathematics to find an objective, value-free method for understanding the world and resolving intersubjective disagreements became the passion of Descartes and of the age he ushered in. For Descartes, the high hopes for mathematization were literally a dream, a mystic three-part dream on the evening of November 10, 1619, in which he believed the secret of nature had been revealed to him. Descartes[2]

> awoke convinced that all of nature is a vast geometrical system. Thereafter he "neither admits nor hopes for any principles in Physics other than those which are in Geometry or in abstract Mathematics, because thus all the phenomena of nature are explained, and some demonstrations of them can be given." Differences among bodies are differences in shape, density, and motion . . . and these properties are real and expressible in mathematical terms. On the other hand, such qualities as color, taste, warmth, and pitch are not real but are reactions of minds to the real, primary qualities. These . . . could be dismissed in an analysis of the real world because they are but illusions. . . . Thus . . . shape . . . and motion in space and time are the source of all properties and are the fundamental realities. In Descartes' words, "give me extension and motion and I will construct the universe.". . . . In brief, the real world is the totality of mathematically expressible motions of objects in space and time, and the entire universe is a great, harmonious, and mathematically designed machine. (pp. 106-107)

For Descartes, mathematics was not merely a useful approach to describing some kinds of knowledge; mathematics was thought of as the key to behavior, because nature itself is mathematical, subject to mathematical laws. Galileo and Bacon spoke of geometry or mathematical principles as the language in which the book of nature is written. Kepler affirmed that mathematical laws are the true causes of events. For these thinkers[3]

> the universe is mathematical in structure and behavior, and nature acts in accordance with inexorable and immutable laws. . . . We can understand now, said Descartes, why mathematical prediction of the future is possible; it is because the mathematical relationships are pre-existing. . . . The mathematical interpretation of nature became so popular and fashionable by 1650 that it spread throughout Europe and dainty, expensively bound

accounts by its chief expositor, Descartes, adorned ladies' dressing tables. (pp. 105, 107)

Two generations after Descartes, Leibniz (cited in Davis & Hersh, 1986, p. 7) sought a "characteristica universalis," a universal objective method to resolve "all human problems, whether of science, law or politics . . . rationally, systematically, by logical computation." Forms of this vision are with us yet in the social sciences and require that mathematization be given priority in the disciplines that study human affairs.

One great hope of this movement was that careful observation and measurement would promote the formation of culture. The careful, dispassionate investigation of the universe was to bring progress to our understanding and experience of daily life. The work of Galileo, Newton, and others of the era enabled remarkable progress on scientific fronts and appeared to many in the 17th and 18th centuries to be facilitated by the concept that the cosmos was essentially a large, well-regulated machine. Alasdair MacIntyre, a professional observer of the effects of the enlightenment, summarized the initial aims of enlightenment thinkers in this way:[4]

> It was the shared belief of the protagonists of the Enlightenment . . . that one and the same set of standards of truth and rationality—indeed of right conduct and adequate aesthetic judgement—was not only available to all human beings qua rational persons, but [these standards] were such that no human being qua rational person could deny their authority. The central project of the Enlightenment was to formulate and to apply those standards. (p. 15)

Thus, the enlightenment claims were initially that there *are* universal standards of truth and right answers to ultimate questions, that these answers are available to everyone through reason with no need for special revelation or other sources of "values" beyond reason, and that these ultimate answers have the force of undeniability (i.e., they "force themselves" on the conversation in a way that cannot be reasonably denied).

Initially it was believed that this conception did not require a prior commitment to an atheistic or naturalistic cosmos. The world's order was viewed as God's own mathematical order, such that the rational study of this order was akin to studying God's own word or intentions. For Descartes, nature's laws are orderly and predictable because of the eternal stability of God's will.[5]

One thing is clear: not only was there in some intellectual leaders a great aspiration to demonstrate that the universe ran like a piece of clockwork, but this was itself initially a religious aspiration. It was felt that there would be something defective in Creation itself . . . unless the whole system of the universe could be shown to be interlocking, so that it carried the pattern of reasonableness and orderliness.[6]

Yet it was not very long until the limits of reason's authority were being pressed by the mainstream of intellectuals. For many, universally accepted standards for all truth and right did *not* seem to be forthcoming from reason. A sharper distinction emerged between the truth, ethics, and beauty that *are* describable and attainable in public discourse through careful observation (such as scientific claims or legal arrangements to protect property), and the values, opinions, and convictions considered private and subjective, and hence awkward for public discourse.[7]

For some, private beliefs seemed to be not merely benign personal relics but capricious and superstitious impediments to careful observation, reason, and advancement. Universal moral truths might exist but directly linking them to our sensory experiences appeared unlikely. Because they could not be empirically verified, skepticism emerged that we have genuine knowledge of them. Hume probably is the best recognized speaker at this turn in the conversation and advocated a straightforward *empiricism* as the direction for intellectual endeavor. Much of the ensuing conversation about data and models departs from a conviction that universal values exist, available through reason and observation; instead, the observable and measurable become the focus of investigation.

This growing emphasis on empirical evidence to the exclusion of other considerations can be associated with a generally *naturalistic* view of the work of science. One well-known observer[8] expressed the skeptical mood that motivated naturalistic empiricism.

Science was born of a faith in the mathematical interpretation of Nature, held long before it had been empirically verified. . . . The turn to experimentation was an anti-rationalist movement, a movement away from the unending and hitherto profitless speculation of a waning religious spirit and away from religious dogmatism so often proved wrong. (p. 109)

D.C. Phillips has pointed out that the phrase "naturalism" suffers from an overabundance of interpretations, from the romantic emphasis on submission to nature, to nonexperimental methods in social science, to various forms of nudism.[9] But our (philosophical) meaning[10] refers to

> a scholar who attempts to explain phenomena that occur within the realm of the physical universe in terms of concepts and explanatory hypotheses that themselves refer to this same "natural" realm; in other words, the naturalist eschews explanations in terms of (literally) super-natural or meta-physical entities. (p. 36)

For scientists operating within this account, there is no God, at least none that matters to our work as scientists and analysts; we are free (in fact, under obligation) to be methodological atheists. Whereas Descartes exempted both God and the human soul from the mathematics of the motion of objects, for many working within the empiricist framework there is strictly deterministic (or possibly probabilistic) causation in the universe. Persons then may be thought of as an element of this deterministic cosmos: our love, our thought and language, our religion, our philanthropy and social orderings are interpreted as expressions of our basic unity with nonhuman nature.

▦ SOME IMPLICATIONS

These themes eventually gave birth to several characteristic ways of engaging in the social and decision sciences. One is the conception that models originate from the raw materials of value-free, objectively measured facts, in which a strong distinction is held between facts and values. For instance, most of modern economic analysis is conducted under the presumption of a strong division of positive from normative issues. Another characteristic habit of the modern social sciences has been the interpretation of love, marriage, education, and altruism as responses that endure because of their survival value; evolutionary drives toward fitness are also seen as forces behind literature, mathematics, humor, or morality.[11]

Marx gave a different but enduring account of the naturalistic forces presumed to be driving human history, with implications for the ways Marxists view human art, morality, work, insanity, law enforcement, literature, religion, accounting, and management science. Skinner and Freud also gave fundamentally naturalistic accounts of human behavior.

And the ascendancy of mathematics in the social sciences in our century is no doubt in part a reflection of mainstream acceptance of some of the naturalistic empiricist worldview. John Stuart Mill and Herbert Spencer are often credited with influencing the human studies in this direction,[12] though a more enduring and fundamental influence was likely the work of Auguste Comte and his account of *positivism*.[13]

Comte's argument[14] that the empiricist methods of natural science can be borrowed by the social sciences begins with the claim that the central methods of science are the only methods that create real knowledge.

> All competent thinkers agree with Bacon that there can be no real knowledge except that which rests upon observed facts. This fundamental maxim is so evidently indisputable if it is applied, as it ought to be, to the mature state of our intelligence. (p. 4)

Comte did not claim that only measurable things could exist or be true but did believe that absolute truth about origins or the "hidden causes" behind the things we sense is unknowable and unobtainable and therefore not worth the search. Thus, for Comte science is limited to the study, through reason and observation, of the regularities or laws that characterize observable phenomena. Sensations, or sense data, are the elements of knowledge on which one may rely, and there is no good reason to think that anything but sensation actually exists.[15] Comte did not accept religious or extrasensory explanations for empirical phenomena, because the ideas in these explanations cannot be justified by the data. Thus, classical positivism encourages religious skepticism. Science might be a means toward generalizing about our sensations, as long as one avoids careless inferences about causes.[16]

By the 1920s and 1930s, classical positivism led to logical positivism, which was especially influential in North America. Logical positivism is best known for advocating the "verifiability principle (or criterion) of meaning." Statements that cannot be verified (and, in principle, refuted) by direct sensory experience are held to be meaningless, and statements are only meaningful if empirically verifiable[17]; if it cannot be sensed, it cannot be discussed. For example, consciousness is not observable but behavior is. Unobservable items cannot be subjected to tests; thus, for a logical positivist, theories about consciousness are unscientific and meaningless but theories about behavior are not. From this perspective verifiable direct sense experience is theory-free, neutral, and foundational, the proper object of science. Even "theories" or models may fail to meet these standards because they may be generalizations that cannot be directly sensed. Some logical positivists were therefore skeptical about the standing of theories as knowledge.

We should point out that, as we are about to see, the label "positivist" is often used too casually and does not include everyone impressed by scientific achievement, nor all those who do numerical research, nor everyone who expects some support for claims that are advanced.

OBJECTIONS TO THE DREAM: ANTIREALISM

The dream of a mathematized analysis transcending personal differences has encountered serious objections since the 1950s, some of which we are about to review. But we should begin by remembering that there always has been an intellectual counterpoint to the dominant theme we have developed so far. Whereas we have been emphasizing the so-called *realist* instinct and its influence in the sciences, there also has been, to varying degrees in different eras, an *antirealist* rejoinder. Instead of tending to view humans as passive observers or sensors, one could tend toward the view that we persons are ourselves the agents who determine the structure and nature of the cosmos.[18]

In this view, things external to the person (such as cars, managers, census data) do exist, but their existence and structure *as these things* is not their own, waiting to be verified; it is granted them by the thought processes of humans. The basic structure of the cosmos is licensed by the way the human mind constitutes that cosmos. Why do we recognize something as "car," rather than merely "3,000 pounds of metal and plastic" or "moving object on smooth surface?" How do we know that a change in shape does not make a car into a noncar but does make a bottle into a vase? Why do we know the difference between "manager" and "worker," when both are, in an objective sense, identical natural items of flesh and blood? What makes some numbers about people "census data," and other similar numbers "anecdotes" or "credit reports" or "attendance figures?"

So for antirealists the fundamental architecture of the world, its space and time; the division of reality into objects and assignment of relevant properties to objects; the divisions between fact, truth, error, and guess; the differences between necessary, sufficient, possible, and probable are distinctions that are not necessarily properties of the cosmos or of things in the cosmos but are the result of human mental creativity. Even the difference between existence and nonexistence might be viewed as a distinction that we humans bring to the world, not something that exists externally that we might discover.

Hence the appellation "antirealist." Without human interpretive activity, there might not be anything true or false, likely or unlikely, limited or abundant, filling space or passing time. Things are not "real" outside of our experience and interpretation of them. Humans are the measure of all things.

And does this mean that there is some "general human consciousness" that structures the world so that we all agree what a "car," "manager," and "census" are, or do we each create our own cosmos? Because numbering elements of reality is an activity of the person, not the cosmos, there may be no good answer to the question, unless one can presume that there are some structures not constructed by the mind that are common to all human minds. Thus, antirealism seems bent toward relativism, not only in what we normally recognize as ethics but in the ways we use and interpret language, manipulate symbols, decide what to do, and model or categorize the world. In the hands of an antirealist, modeling might be thought of not as a means of discovery but of self-expression (or, for skeptics, manipulation); statistical methods might be tools not of learning but of advocacy.[19]

Now that realism and antirealism have been introduced, consider how differently the two views think about objectivity and subjectivity. The realist tradition has thought of knowledge as something that is built up from either our uninterpreted experience of the world (like sense data) or our ability to reason. We then aim to form generalizations around the dispassionate observation of these objects, withholding judgment and keeping our natural likes and dislikes out of the way. An objective view of the external reality develops from the professional community, outside ourselves, relatively unscathed by our own framework or preferences. Here there is an attempt to establish a basis for truth that is independent of persons, intersubjective but beyond or without personality.

But for a person with antirealist instincts, there is no fundamental external reality for us to confront with reason or observation. Observation itself is motivated by a prior ordering of the world, and it is difficult to see how these prior orderings can be challenged by evidence when the theory itself determines which evidence counts.

▨ DISAPPOINTMENTS WITH THE DREAM

Whereas both positivism and various forms of antirealism have competed for the attention of the social sciences, it is clear that in the long run positivism has been more influential. The grand program envisioned by Descartes and Leibniz was influential in the formation of the modern social sciences. And much of the empirical work in the social and decision sciences, represented in most mathematical methods textbooks and in the work of most practitioners, still operates as if it were the value-free confrontation between theories and objective facts, by which we are led ever more deeply into truth.[20]

Yet much of the perceptual psychology and philosophy of science underlying Descartes's and Leibniz's program is considered discredited even by those who are not antirealists, especially among the last two generations,[21] though much of the practice of the social sciences has not yet responded to these developments. To complete this chapter of introductions to the conversation about just how values, data, and models should interact in the social sciences, we present some basic notes about the decline of positivism as an intellectual force. We do this by briefly considering the work of Thomas Kuhn and Karl Popper.[22] After discussing the contributions of these two leading critics of positivism, we will be in a much stronger position in the rest of the book to consider how best to approach the principled use of data and models in the human and social sciences.

▨ POSTPOSITIVISM

Popper is known for his advocacy of a so-called nonfoundationalist attitude toward what humans can claim to know. Along with Popper, many would agree that there is no absolutely dependable foundation within human thought—not reason, not empiricism—for the claims we make, such that one could be so certain of a position that all opportunity for changing one's mind in the future would be rejected. In particular, sense experience is not a solid foundation, as it is influenced by the very theories we hope to challenge with it. All of our claims to know something must be tentative.[23]

> The question about the sources of our knowledge . . . has always been asked in the spirit of: "What are the best sources of our knowledge—the most

reliable ones, those which will not lead us into error, and those to which we can and must turn, in case of doubt, as the last court of appeal?" I propose to assume, instead, that no such ideal sources exist—no more than ideal rules—and that all "sources" are liable to lead us into error at times. And I propose to replace, therefore, the question of the sources of our knowledge by the entirely different question: "How can we hope to detect and eliminate error?" (p. 25)

This is not to say that there is no truth outside ourselves to be discovered. In responding to those idealists who emphasize that theories are developed by fallible analysts, Popper argued that there is indeed a truth outside the observer to be discovered and that theories should aim to be true descriptions of the external world and its regularities.[24]

[Theories should be] genuine conjectures—highly informative guesses about the world which although not verifiable (i.e., capable of being shown true) can be submitted to severe critical tests. They are serious attempts to discover the truth . . . even though we do not know, and may perhaps never know, whether it is true or not. . . . Theories are our own inventions. . . . This has been clearly seen by the idealist. But some of these theories of ours can clash with reality; and when they do, we know that there is a reality; that there is something to remind us of the fact that our ideas may be mistaken. And this is why the realist is right. (pp. 115, 117)

Yet Popper admitted the difficulty of knowing whether we have actually discovered something that is true.[25]

The status of truth in the objective sense, as correspondence to the facts, and its role as a regulative principle, may be compared to that of a mountain peak which is permanently, or almost permanently, wrapped in clouds. The climber may not merely have difficulties in getting there—he may not know when he gets there, because he may be unable to distinguish, in the clouds, between the main summit and some subsidiary peak. Yet this does not affect the objective existence of the summit. . . . The very idea of error, or of doubt . . . implies the idea of an objective truth which we may fail to reach. (p. 226)

Thus, one may not know if one is really near the truth, but the possibility of being nearer or farther away still can serve as a *regulative principle or ideal.* There is no use giving up and concluding that any claim is as good as any other. Some claims are more warranted than others.

If our preconceptions and theories always color our observations, then what is the best the community of scholars can do in judging which claims are nearest the truth? Popper argues that scientific claims must be *falsifiable*. It is no use inductively putting together generalizations or theories from sources (like reason or data) that were alleged to provide a firm foundation; better to pay relatively little attention to the *sources* of the theories and instead turn attention to whether their implications are testable and, if so, whether these tests falsify the claim being made.[26] For Popper, this is the only kind of inquiry that can qualify as science.[27]

> So my answer to the questions "How do you know? What is the source or basis of your assertion? What observations have led you to it?" would be "I do not know; my assertion was merely a guess. Never mind the source, or the sources, from which it may spring. . . . But if you are interested in the problem which I tried to solve by my tentative assertion, you may help me by criticizing it as severely as you can." (p. 53)

In fact, too much concern with justifying the basis of scientific work actually may be harmful.[28]

> We cannot rob the scientist of his partisanship without also robbing him of his humanity, and we cannot suppress or destroy his value judgments without destroying him as a human being and as a scientist. Our motives and even our purely scientific ideals . . . are deeply anchored in extra-scientific and, in part, in religious valuations. Thus the "objective" or the "value-free" scientist is hardly the ideal scientist. (p. 97)

For Popper, objectivity is not within the ability of any individual. Objectivity is a characteristic of the group rather than the individual; it is the result of the process of submitting one's work to critical review by peers. It is to be pursued in the context of justifying or falsifying results, not the context of discovering or proposing new approaches.[29]

So, Popper's nonfoundationalist ideas and his realism lead to an emphasis on falsifiability.[30] This attempt to falsify theories has the unfortunate potential to catch us in a circular trap: It is clear that the theories scientists hold will influence their decisions about which data are counted as relevant to science. Theories direct the scientist's attention toward some topics and measures, away from others. Then if a particular theory becomes the convention of a scientific community, practitioners' attention might be directed away from data that would falsify the mainstream theory. These nonconformist data become "outliers" or "noise" in the data set, or the data that would falsify the theory may never be generated in the first place. The profession can fall into a "groupthink" culture that reinforces itself through its professional standards. Thus data alone, analyzed without considering the professional context that generates them, cannot be the rock-bottom arbitrators between believable and unbelievable.

This leads to the importance of Thomas Kuhn's work. If data actually provided a solid foundation for scientific work, one would expect knowledge to grow slowly through the layering of discovery and theorizing. But actual science is dynamic, subject to fits and starts; theories are overthrown, old data are reinterpreted in new ways.[31]

Kuhn interpreted this dynamism of science as an interplay between *normal* and *revolutionary* science. The scientific community usually does its normal science within some particular mental framework that directs one's attention to certain concepts, data, and problems. Data are not pure sense stimuli but are the result of a process of classification and measurement. Data are judged useful, and theories are judged fruitful or nonfalsified, relative to a current set of presumptions in the discipline, a latent consensus regarding which data are relevant to which questions, which regularities require explanation, which things are natural order and which others are deviations, and which assumptions and questions are reasonable. Data that do not confirm the current paradigm or that would falsify part of it may not enter the discussion. Thus, theories carry with them a worldview, a *Weltanschauung* that colors one's judgment about the presumptions, interests, and framework of other theories.

Scientific revolutions—changes from one kind of normal science to another—occur when there is a *paradigm shift*. The fundamental way in which the community views the world changes; the concepts, data, and problems that preoccupy the community are altered. Revolutions are normally triggered by the admission of events that cannot easily be reconciled with the current paradigm of normal science. The professional consensus about the conventional paradigm erodes, the community endures a period under several competing paradigms, and a new candidate for consensus emerges. The new paradigm is expected to be logically incompatible with the former consensus, generally involving different values and standards. In effect, one *Weltanschauung* is replaced by another.[32] "Scientific revolutions are . . . those non-cumulative developmental episodes in which an older paradigm is replaced in whole or in part by an incompatible new one."[33]

So Kuhn is clearly not a positivist; science is ultimately more a matter of persuasion than of observation and proof. Is he therefore an antirealist? Can anyone step outside one's own paradigm to critically view the world through a different one? One might argue that, if different paradigms were incommensurable, with our meanings depending in a radical way on our paradigm, we would each be trapped in our own judgments, values, and standards. These would be nearly unchallengeable from within the paradigm. No paradigm could be judged superior, because such judgments and even the language of observation must be made from within some paradigm. There would be no neutral observation language, set of questions to be answered, or standard for good science in the face of identical phenomena. If different paradigms were not mutually intelligible, it would not make sense to ask which is more persuasive about a given point; each paradigm would be left with its own truth.

This kind of absolute relativism seems unpersuasive to many[34] and bears a difficult burden of proof. It must show that, unlike everything else, it is true for everybody. Kuhn appears not to be such a relativist. Two practitioners with different paradigms see different things when looking at the same event, but there is a real event to be observed, and in practice there exist large shared vocabularies across paradigms to describe the event. "Though the world does not change with a change of paradigm, the scientist afterwards works in a different world."[35]

Nevertheless, Kuhn's work has sometimes been presented as an antirealist approach to the social sciences. This may be due to his initially loose use of the word "paradigm." Though it is the central concept in Kuhn's thesis, several reviewers have pointed out that he uses it in 21 different ways, some of which are not mutually consistent.[36] Some uses correspond to a *Weltanschauung*, whereas others clearly do not.[37] Thus,

> The truth of the thesis that shared paradigms are (or are behind) the common factors guiding scientific research appears to be guaranteed . . . by the breadth of the term "paradigm". . . . Kuhn's view is made to appear convincing only by inflating the definition of "paradigm" until that term becomes so vague and ambiguous that it cannot easily be withheld, so general that it cannot easily be applied, and so misleading that it is a positive hindrance to the understanding of some central aspects of science.[38]

Kuhn responded by indicating that the unfortunate term "paradigm" blended two separate notions: *exemplars* and *disciplinary matrixes*. Exemplars are particular instances of work accepted by the scientific community as models for how a particular subject should be approached. Disciplinary matrixes are the shared items that allow professionals to communicate clearly and reach a professional consensus. These include shared symbols, values, and beliefs in exemplars.

Normal science, therefore, proceeds within a common disciplinary matrix or *Weltanschauung*. Though it cannot be fully stated, it would include ideas about how the basic items in the world interact with each other and with our senses and measurement instruments, what questions are important about these items, and what methods are appropriate in pursuing these questions. Students learn this matrix by studying the part of it that is easily made explicit and archetypical, the exemplars. Exemplars are well-known, characteristic applications of the community's theories to the community's subject; they give the community its archetypes and metaphors for how good scientific work is done.

A scientific revolution is a shift of thinking, in which factions of practitioners begin to hold up new exemplars as the archetypes of good science. This leads the revolutionary factions to prize different questions, cite different data, form a different disciplinary language, and in general hold different professional values. A full revolution occurs when the entire community embraces the new disciplinary matrix, with different research agendas, language, values, and standards.

A revolution may not happen automatically just because a new theory fits some observations more closely than the old theory. The new theory still may be judged to raise less significant questions, give less substantial answers, or be less fruitful in advancing the discipline. The new theory may not become a convincing model or archetype of how to engage in productive science.

FROM PRINCIPLES TO PRACTICE

We have argued that the practice of the social and human sciences still is heavily influenced by positivism, even though the basic hallmarks of positivism have been discredited. In raising questions about positivism, Popper and Kuhn have explored intermediate positions between classical positivism and antirealism. Our discussion has reviewed several themes that have gained currency with the decline of positivism: Though claims of truth in the social and human sciences must be somewhat tentative, objectivity still can serve as a regulative principle toward which one strives. In pursuing objectivity, we should pay special attention to the process through which ideas are established and error is identified and eliminated. Throughout the process, one must remain open to the possibility that the entire framework of analysis may be misdirecting one's attention.

How could the daily work of practitioners incorporate these themes? This is a question we pursue in the rest of the book. We will walk step-by-step through the information cycle, seeking at each point to make a beginning in sifting the practices and habits of the social and human sciences.

▨ NOTES

1. Marsden (1994).
2. Kline (1953).
3. Kline (1953).
4. Quoted in Neuhaus (1990). For a full discussion of MacIntyre's views on the topic, see MacIntyre (1981, Chapters 4 and 5) or MacIntyre (1988, Chapter 12).
5. Kline (1953, p. 108).
6. Butterfield (1957, p. 119).
7. See, for example, Kant (1785/1959) for a classic rendition of the connection between the public reason of scholarship and the private reason of the religious sphere.
8. Kline (1953).
9. Phillips (1992, p. 36).
10. Phillips (1992).
11. See, for example, Bergstrom (1995, p. 58).
12. See, for example, Mill (Sixth book, Chapter 3, cited in Phillips, 1992) and Spencer (1855).
13. We will discuss Comte, Popper, and Kuhn in some detail in this chapter. For each we try to outline his conception of the method, scope, and source of knowledge of science.
14. Comte (1868/1970).
15. See, for example, Miller (1985, p. 106).
16. There is some circularity in the reasoning here. Because we cannot directly sense or experience theories, laws, and generalizations, a classical positivist should have some skepticism about the possibility that theories are a legitimate subject of science. Yet Comte made such generalizations the aim of science, perhaps as a shorthand way to refer to direct sensory experience—what we might call "operational definitions." John Dewey and William James approached this problem by arguing that we *can* directly experience theories and generalizations and "possible" objects; these are not mere constructions.
17. Or, in the case of math and logic, statements can be meaningful if they are analytic.

18. Kant's (1781/1965) *Critique of Pure Reason* is sometimes identified as a modern genesis of this view, though, as always, identifying any particular person as an antirealist will raise objections by some.

19. It is possible to recognize the antirealist voice in some schools within the social and decision sciences. Richard Rorty has emerged as a contemporary widely read popularizer of some of these approaches. Some forms of "advocacy research," scholarship that seeks support for the advocacy of some group or cause, also are in debt to antirealism. And, as we shall see in Chapter 5, the approach to measurement that characterizes much of psychometrics has a highly antirealist flavor.

20. One might offer the interest in qualitative research as a counterexample, but our reading is that qualitative researchers are concerned that careful observation be done (rather than "roughriding" into a situation with too easy generalizations) and that appropriate measurement indexes be relied on (rather than forcing every trait to be represented by a cardinal scale). Qualitative researchers still may be giving too little attention to the weaknesses of positivism.

21. One wonders why this situation of professional inertia surrounding discredited ideas persists. One explanation argues that positivism has been "institutionalized," as the philosopher of science Hillary Putnam puts it. We suspect this is partly because of the use to which social science has been put by the institutions of public policy since the 1950s (see Chapter 9) and partly because positivist methods grant more cumulative knowledge than the more interpretive alternatives. There also may be financial incentives in favor of positivism, such as the rationalization of business activities it allows and promotes. This is probably clearest when it takes the form of computer technologies.

22. A helpful discussion of these authors is spread throughout Phillips' (1992) book.

23. Popper (1968).

24. Popper (in Lewis, 1953, pp. 115, 117).

25. Popper (1953, p. 226).

26. Popper's emphasis on falsifiability is sometimes countered with the Duhemian hypothesis that is discussed in Chapter 7: In practice, any test of a particular theory requires simultaneous reliance on a host of other assumptions and theories; if the experiment appears to falsify the theory, we cannot really be sure if the primary theory should be rejected or if one of the collateral theories or assumptions is at fault. Thus, any theory might be "insulated" from falsifiability.

27. Popper (in Miller, 1985, p. 53).

28. Popper (1976).

29. We might add here that, because falsification of a theory is possible but confirmation is not, Popper argues it is unwise for a community to hold one mainstream theory and exclude all others. Many conjectures or theories should mark the scientific community. For Popper, this is how science progresses—not through the gradual inclusion of new observations under an expanding orthodox theory but by testing many competing conjectures. The terms used by one theory can still be understood within other theoretical frameworks and by practitioners who do not accept the theory, and at least some questions are straightforward true-or-false issues; so theories can be compared and falsified by experiments, and knowledge can grow.

30. This is not to say, with the logical positivists, that nonfalsifiable claims are meaningless. They still may be true, but they are not science, because they are not subject to

falsification; they cannot enter the process by which we authorize a conclusion as "objective," that is, warranted because it has not yet been falsified. So an idea can be true but not objective, because it is not scientific. An idea also could be scientific and objective (not yet falsified) but prove later to be untrue. Neither objective (falsifiable) nor subjective (nonfalsifiable) ideas are necessarily closer to the truth, but at least objective ones can be submitted to a rigorous review process that seems to give them a wider warrant.

31. Data also fail as the ultimate foundation for some science because scientific theories extend to unobservable realities (like subatomic structures).

32. We might wonder whether, in the social and decision sciences, there is a drawable distinction between normal and revolutionary science. Does "normal" science ever occur with a broad consensus on the discipline's scope and methods, or are social and decision sciences in a state of perpetual pluralism, not cumulatively achieving closure on basic paradigm questions? If the latter, then Popper's hope, that a large number of conjectures should mark a scientific community, is fulfilled, and the need for Kuhnian consensus-revolutions is partly overcome.

33. Kuhn (1962, p. 91).

34. See, for example, Newton-Smith (1981) or Siegel (1987).

35. Kuhn (1962, p. 120). See also p. 128 or Section X.

36. See, for example, Masterman (1970) or Shapere (1964).

37. See, for example, Suppes (1974, p. 136).

38. Shapere (1964, pp. 384-395).

THE INFORMATION CYCLE

Our topic is principles that ought to guide the collection and use of human information. In Part I we focused on "theoretical" aspects of our topic: Chapter 1 discussed the scope of human information, several critical problems with its use, and how we planned to proceed. Chapter 2 introduced the fundamental notion of "model" that underlies the entire process of collecting and organizing data. Chapter 3 outlined a historical context for understanding the use of data and models as a means to obtain knowledge.

Our goal for Part II is to apply the approach to norms introduced in Chapter 1—combining limitations of methodology with contextual norms—to develop some helpful normative principles for the collection and use of human information. We use the information cycle as an organizing framework for examining a broad range of uses of data and models, from the earliest stage of question formulation to the final stage of decision making and policy formation. Chapter 4 focuses primarily on the values and assumptions implicit in the use of data and models. This issue underlies the first two steps of the information cycle—identifying a need for information and formulating a precise question. Chapters 5 and 6 explore measurement, the third step of the information cycle. We will not spend time on steps 4 and 5—data collection and exploratory data analysis—but, rather, refer the reader to some excellent work that has already addressed that aspect of the cycle.[1] Chapter 7 addresses the next step, formulation and testing hypotheses, especially the interpretation of relationships that are inferred statistically. Chapter 8 also discusses interpretation, as we look at causal explanations in the social sciences. Chapter 9 examines the last two steps in the information cycle—the promulgation of results and, especially, policy formation.

NOTE

1. For an excellent outline of the ethical principles that should guide these two steps, see the article by Warwick and Pettigrew (1983).

A Priori *Influences on the Information Cycle*

A homeowner walking to his garden with spade in hand may not notice the peeling paint on a bench. But he is far more likely to notice the peeling if he were carrying a paint brush and paint can. His choice of spade or brush exerts a substantial influence on what he perceives and how he responds to that perception.

The first two steps of the information cycle are identifying a need for information and formulating a precise question. Several factors influence the conduct of these steps. Some of these factors are highly individual and personal, some may be shared by professionals or other communities, and some may be shared by entire cultures or subcultures. An individual's purpose is one such factor. For example, imagine an artist, an environmental scientist, and a geologist each preparing to carry out his or her professional tasks in the same mountain setting. The information each would want, the questions each would ask, and, hence, their perceptions would be quite different.

Prior understandings also can influence perception; such understandings can be individual or communal. For instance, a white, male social worker recently was walking down the second-floor corridor of a neighborhood

community center in Grand Rapids, Michigan. He glanced outside, saw
what he perceived to be two young African American men fighting on the
basketball court, and filed an "incident report." An African American,
female social worker, when she heard about the incident report, com-
mented that she had been walking down the first-floor corridor at that
same instant and also had seen the men on the basketball court. But to her,
they were simply "blowing off steam." In reflecting on the situation later,
the second social worker suggested that their different cultural back-
grounds led one of them to observe hostility when the other observed
playfulness. Because of the difference, the first social worker perceived a
need to create human information—namely, the incident report—whereas
the other did not. And the kinds of questions he sought to address in his
report were generated by his perception of hostility.

Belief systems are another *a priori* influence on what we perceive and
the questions we ask. By a "belief system" we mean a complex combination
of assumptions and values that influence many aspects of a person,
including perceptions and behavior. Belief systems can be quite explicit and
carefully articulated, as in some systems of religious belief, or they can be
implicit and not clearly formulated, as in some social movements.[1] But in
either case, they exert a substantial influence on how social phenomena are
perceived. For instance, Freudians tend to interpret social phenomena in
terms of repressed desires. Marxists look for evidence of class conflict.
Feminists tend to perceive social phenomena in terms of patterns of thought
and social structures that typify genders. Christians tend to look for
evidence of human sinfulness and possibilities for redemption. And many
thinkers have developed belief systems that combine elements from more
than one system and that influence their questions and perceptions in
complex ways.

We focus in this chapter on a particular set of factors that act as *a priori*
influences on the information cycle: the modes of thinking characteristic
of various scientific methodologies, the "intellectual tools" that the social
science gardener carries. These methods are widely used and, as we saw in
Chapter 3, have exerted a strong formative influence on Western culture;
subsequently they have influenced many other cultures as well. Thus, it is
important as we begin our study of the information cycle to understand
how they influence our perceptions and our questions.

We have identified three modes of thinking that are widely used in the
social and decision sciences. The first is empirical methods—the use of
careful observations to study "what is." This mode is what is most com-

monly thought of as "social science." We call the second mode "structural analysis." Briefly, it is the use of mathematics to study "what might be" rather than "what is." The third mode is often called "normative decision making," although "normative" is used differently in this phrase than in the rest of this book. Normative decision making involves elements of both structural analysis and empirical approaches and other features.

We have five objectives for this chapter: (a) to explain each mode of thinking and its potential benefits, (b) to analyze its underlying assumptions and values, (c) to examine how the underlying assumptions and values of each mode of thinking can influence an investigator's perceptions of the need for information and the questions formulated, (d) to examine some potential problems in applying each mode (and hence its underlying assumptions and values) to social phenomena, and (e) to ask what principles ought to guide the use of these modes of thinking in the social sciences.

EMPIRICAL METHODS

In this section we consider the assumptions and values inherent in empirical science. We begin by illustrating the methodology with a familiar example: Ivan P. Pavlov's work on conditioned reflexes, perhaps the most famous work in the history of psychology.

Pavlov was a physiologist, not a psychologist. He had used dogs to study the role of salivation in digestion. He observed dogs salivating before food or even the odor of food was presented to them. This was behavior that could not be explained by physiology alone. After observing this behavior, Pavlov hypothesized that the dogs had learned to expect food in response to certain signals, such as the sound of footsteps. He distinguished *unconditioned* or *automatic reflexes* from *conditioned* or *learned reflexes* and sought to understand how the latter are acquired. He designed a carefully controlled laboratory that was completely soundproofed and isolated the dogs from the experimenters and from all extraneous stimuli during the experimental procedures. He found that he could condition the dogs to respond with salivation to several neutral stimuli—the sound of a metronome, the odor of vanilla, and the sight of a rotating object. In fact,

The theory of classical conditioning (also called Pavlovian conditioning) is universally accepted and has remained virtually unchanged since its conception through Pavlov's work. It is used to explain and interpret a wide range of human behavior, including where phobias come from, why you dislike certain foods, the source of your emotions, how advertising works, why you feel anxiety before a job interview, and what arouses you sexually.[2]

Pavlov's work is one of the classical studies on which the field of psychology rests. Many studies have followed up on his work.

Pavlov's research illustrates many potential benefits of the classic methods of empirical science. Unfortunately, as we shall see, many of these benefits are difficult to obtain in much of the social sciences. Empirical science is an effective tool for understanding replicable situations, grounding that understanding in careful observations rather than in speculation. It provides a strong basis for intersubjective agreement through the persuasiveness of the controlled experiment, provides explanatory and predictive power in routine situations, enables the identification of anomalies (as it makes clear what is routinely expected), and explicitly lays out its methods for critical scrutiny.

Pavlov's work also illustrates several of the traditional assumptions and values that underlie empirical investigation.

■   The investigation is concerned with routine aspects of situations, that is, situations in which replicable (not unique) events occur.

■   A focus on one or perhaps a small number of aspects does not result in any essential misrepresentation of the situation.

■   Scientific language (i.e., language characterized by precise, explicit definition and logical reasoning) can represent the situation faithfully.

■   "Truth" is a property of statements and means that statements accurately correspond to reality.

■   Greater precision in measurement and language means greater truthfulness.

■   Prediction and control are both possible and desirable.

■   The situation operates according to the ordinary understanding of cause and effect, perhaps extended to include probabilistic notions of causation. (We will expand on this notion in Chapter 8, but briefly, this means that principles expressed in terms of hypotheses and conclusions can tell us what outcome(s) to expect when particular conditions occur.)

■   Knowledge can be obtained by an interaction between careful observation and theory formation. In this interaction, theories are hypothesized and conclusions deduced from them. Generalizations are also induced from observations.[3] The conclusions and generalizations are compared and differences lead to improvement in the theories.

■ The ordinary laws of reasoning apply—noncontradiction (an unambiguous statement and its negation cannot both be true) and the law of the excluded middle (an unambiguous statement is either true or its negation is true)—and when used with true statements lead to conclusions that are also true.

■ The researcher is not advocating an agenda. He or she has only one purpose: to provide grounds for accepting or rejecting the research hypothesis with no other (perhaps hidden) purposes that may affect the results.

Two additional values, historically important for empirical investigation but not illustrated by Pavlov's work, are (a) if two theories account equally well for observations, the simpler is preferable, and (b) theories ought to be organized axiomatically, that is, in terms of a minimal set of carefully articulated fundamental principles.

Thus, a psychologist with a Pavlovian orientation seeks understanding through carefully controlled experiments, looks for conditioned reflexes (hence all of the examples given above of phenomena that have been "explained" by conditioned reflexes), approaches psychological phenomena through the study of repeatable rather than unique events, looks for the same type of cause and effect commonly used in the natural sciences, and so forth.

Let's briefly consider an example of social research, Emile Durkheim's classic work on suicide. Durkheim is generally regarded as the father of sociology in part because of this work. We will examine Durkheim's investigation in more detail in Chapter 5, but for now we can summarize a few main features. Durkheim collected data on the frequency of suicide in several European countries and provinces. He observed that the frequencies were remarkably consistent from year to year and that Protestant countries had significantly higher suicide rates than Catholic countries. In fact, Protestant and Catholic provinces within the same country showed the same pattern of having higher suicide rates for Protestants. After investigating many possible explanations for this difference, Durkheim hypothesized that the critical factor was "social integration" and reasoned that married people would have a significantly lower suicide rate than single people. When he compared suicide rates for married and single people, he found that the data confirmed his expectation and thus Durkheim concluded that social integration was indeed the critical factor.

Suicide is a complex phenomenon. In studying it scientifically, Durkheim made many simplifying assumptions: He focused on a replicable, measurable aspect of suicide, the frequency of its occurrence. This one aspect was studied apart from complex issues, such as the impact of the suicides on the surviving family members. Considerable care also was exercised to be sure the rates were accurate and that the differences were not due to factors such as differing standards for whether to record a death as suicide. Many hypotheses for the observed difference in rates were advanced, tested, and rejected before the hypothesis of social integration was found to enable correct predictions. Careful reasoning was used and logical inconsistencies avoided. And as far as we know, the only agenda that Durkheim pursued in this study was the advancement of knowledge. In short, Durkheim could use scientific methodology by simplifying a complex situation, focusing on one aspect that fit the assumptions on which empirical investigation is based. Thus, we have the same situation we saw in Chapter 2 with any use of modeling—it provides a helpful and useful simplification of a situation, but it always leaves some things out and has to be interpreted in the original, larger context. Durkheim's work was, in fact, extraordinarily helpful, and the hypothesis of social integration as a significant factor has subsequently been used to assess many social phenomena. Note, however, that it does, in a sense, misrepresent suicide, in that focus on its frequency obscures its tragedy. But certainly under the simplifying assumptions Durkheim made, the phenomena he studied fit the assumptions and values of empirical science well.

It is not hard to add many examples of social phenomena that partially fit the underlying assumptions of empirical investigation. A few examples are demographic factors, economic activity (such as prices for a particular commodity in a particular area over time), use of various modes of travel, human reaction times, and the relationship between people's reported religious beliefs and their voting behavior.

Nevertheless, some important social phenomena do not fit these assumptions. Let's consider each assumption.

■ Social phenomena are often not replicable. A researcher cannot say "Let's rerun the last economic quarter with some different parameters this time and see what changes." The social researcher is often forced to take "snapshots" at particular moments in time and hope that no undetected but significant changes have affected the characteristics being studied. We'll return to this point in Chapter 7.

■ In many social situations there are many variables, most of them uncontrollable. The controlled experiment is an ideal in the social sciences that is rarely attainable.[4] A social researcher always must focus on a small number of variables and risk misrepresenting the larger situation.

■ Language is finite and social phenomena are typically more complex than we can grasp. Thus, we always must simplify and, again, risk misrepresenting at least to some extent. Also, languages of metaphor, story, music, and the visual arts may represent many social phenomena more effectively than scientific language. Consider, for example, *The Diary of Anne Frank*. No amount of data can communicate the meaning of the Nazi era as effectively.

■ A view of truth as statements that correspond to reality is helpful, but by itself it is insufficient for understanding many social phenomena. For example, someone studying friendship relationships has at best a limited understanding of friendship without having been a friend. Also, many scholars argue that in gender and ethnic studies, one cannot fully grasp what it means to be female or African American in the United States unless one is female or African American. Without such experiences, even a careful investigator can inadvertently make false assumptions, overlook significant factors, and miss nuances. Truth-in-being as well as truth-as-correspondence can add a great deal to one's understanding.

■ Control is not always desirable—for instance, one frequent criticism of B.F. Skinner's *Beyond Freedom and Dignity*[5] was that it advocated an excessive level of social control.

■ Cause and effect explanations of social phenomena do not take human intentionality into account. But many scholars argue that human intentionality must be considered as well. We will return to this point in Chapter 8.

■ Any work in the natural or social sciences requires sorting through many variables and requires insight and interpretation, for example, Durkheim's hypothesis that social integration was the key factor in understanding the frequency of suicide. But the role of interpretation is especially acute in the social sciences for at least these two following reasons:

1. Social phenomena normally involve many variables that cannot be controlled. Hence, judgments must be made about which factors are likely to be important.

2. The results of social investigation often directly affect human beings and thus cannot be considered apart from their ethical implications. Although even in the natural sciences, the knowledge obtained by observation and theory cannot be separated from interpretation, this linkage is more immediate in the social sciences.

■ Because social phenomena are complex and poorly understood, they are typically studied via proxies (for example, gross domestic product is a proxy for economic well-being). A proxy is often chosen because it is measurable. But greater precision in the measurement of a proxy does not necessarily give a more truthful representation of the actual phenomena in question—such truthfulness depends on the appropriateness of the proxy.

■ Whereas some writers question the ordinary rules of logic when applied to social phenomena,[6] we do not. In fact, we do not see how meaningful thought is possible without them. Nevertheless, even if such laws are accepted, they only enable us to uncover contradictions in the assumptions we have formulated or to work out the implications of these assumptions. Thus, the effectiveness of rules of reasoning still depends on our insight into the phenomena and our skill in articulating these insights as hypotheses.

■ A new mode of research called "advocacy research" has become increasingly popular. In advocacy research, a scholar specifically seeks data and analyses what will advance a particular cause. The cause is not hidden—the scholar is totally honest about his or her advocacy—but such a scholar is certainly not the disinterested observer of classical science. In fact, many argue that all research is really advocacy research and that scholars who declare themselves advocacy researchers are simply being more forthcoming about their commitments than ones who do not.

■ The social sciences have not been notably successful in developing theories that lend themselves to axiomatic organization.

The critical question that must be asked at this point is, "How can we know which aspects of social phenomena lend themselves to empirical methods and which do not?" Unfortunately, we have not found a satisfactory answer to this question beyond referring to the empirical methods' assumptions themselves: Can replicable features be identified? Can helpful, unambiguous categories be identified? Can the situation be faithfully represented by a small number of variables? And so forth. But it is clear that some essential questions, such as "Is the variable I am focusing on important?" and "What is the significance of this result in the larger context of the situation?" require insight and interpretation from outside the scientific process.

In conclusion, the social sciences differ in fundamental ways from the natural sciences. The social scientist is indeed as much a genuine scientist as any physicist, chemist, or biologist. Nevertheless, because the interpretive aspect is so much more explicit than it is in the natural sciences, the image of Galileo dropping objects of different mass from the Tower of Pisa is not an appropriate model for social scientists to emulate. Rather, the social scientist is more like Sherlock Holmes, carefully gathering data to investigate unique events over which he had no control. Visions of a positive social science and a "social physics" are unattainable, because so many social phenomena do not satisfy the assumptions of empirical science. This does not mean that scientific techniques, such as careful observation, measurement, and inference ought to be rejected in the social sciences. Rather, the social scientist must be constantly vigilant about whether the situation being studied can be modeled to fit the assumptions of science without grossly misrepresenting it. Social scientific results also must be interpreted in terms of the complex social context within which they arose. Thus, the standard of persuasiveness in the social sciences is different from that of the natural sciences. The standard is the compelling explanation that takes all of the data into account and explicitly involves interpretation rather than the controlled experiment. The goals of investigation are also different—the creation of such compelling explanations rather than the formation of nomothetic laws.

STRUCTURAL ANALYSIS

Users of empirical methods seek to understand the world through careful observation; they study "what is." Users of structural analysis, on the other hand, begin with some facts about the real world but then represent and experiment with abstract ideas that may or may not ultimately become concrete realities in the real world; they study "what might be."

One excellent example of structural analysis is Kenneth Arrow's (1921 -) impossibility theorem. This result was first proven in 1950, although

Arrow's original paper had some minor errors that were corrected later. Arrow received the Nobel Prize in Economics in 1972, at least in part for this result. The theorem addresses the issue of fairness in group decision making. As such, it is important in economics, sociology, and political science. The proof is not difficult to understand—its genius lies in the brilliant clarity with which the theorem is formulated.

For instance, suppose a five-member committee is faced with a collection of three alternative proposals to choose among. And suppose each of the five decision makers ranks the three alternatives from highest to lowest according to his or her own preferences. These five individual lists then could be consolidated into a single composite list. Not only would this process produce a "winner," but all of the alternatives would be given a ranking that is supposed to represent a consensus of the group.

Arrow generalized this example to an arbitrary number of individuals and alternatives. He asked, "What should characterize a fair consolidation process, assuming that each committee member has one vote?" Stated informally, the properties Arrow listed are the following:[7]

1. There should be no *a priori* restrictions on the rankings. That is, each decision maker should be free to rank the alternatives in any order.

2. If all decision makers rank an alternative, *a*, above an alternative, *b*, the consolidated list should place *a* above *b*.

3. If one or more alternatives are removed from consideration, the relative rankings of the remaining alternatives in the consolidated list should not change.

4. If the consolidated list ranks *a* above *b*, and a decision maker who ranked *b* above *a* changes so as to rank *a* above *b*, the new consolidated list should still rank *a* above *b*.

5. There is no dictator.

Arrow then proved that there can be no systematic consolidation process that satisfies all five properties. This is a phenomenal result! It is a social science counterpart to the natural science law that there can be no perpetual motion machines—that is, just as there can be no perfectly efficient machine, so there can be no perfectly fair voting procedure, when there are more than two candidates.[8] Note that Arrow does **not** say that all instances of combining individual voter's preferences into a group preference ranking are unfair. Rather, he says that for any consolidation procedure, there is always some situation in which it will appear unfair by violating at least one of the above properties. Thus, just as the nonexistence of a perpetual motion machine does not stop engineers from trying to improve efficiency, this theorem should not stop us from trying to find fairer procedures. Rather, it tells us that a perfect procedure is unattainable.

A second example of structural analysis is Banzhaf's power index—a technique for allocating votes in a weighted voting situation. For instance, county legislatures typically consist of representatives from towns with different populations. How can power be allocated fairly? One approach might be to give each town a number of votes proportional to its population. But this may leave larger towns with the ability to determine the outcome of all decisions, in effect disenfranchising all of the smaller towns. A different approach to allocating votes was devised by John Banzhaf, a lawyer, in 1965.[9] He devised a technique for measuring power in a legislature and then suggested that votes should be assigned to towns so that their power, not their number of votes, is proportional to their population.

Suppose a particular assignment of votes is being tested for fairness. (For an example, see Figure 4.1.) Banzhaf's index requires us to look at all possible winning coalitions of legislators. If a particular legislator can change that coalition from winning to losing by withdrawing, that legislator is "critical." Banzhaf's index defines the power of a legislator to be the number of coalitions in which that legislator is critical, divided by the total number of times any legislator is critical. Thus, Banzhaf's index provides a precise definition of voting power and a way to measure power in any weighted voting situation. The measure of power does not depend on any empirical data but only on how the voting rules are structured.

Arrow's theorem and Banzhaf's index illustrate several characteristics of structural analysis. Perhaps the most critical point is that structural analysis is not empirical. It models abstract properties of a situation rather than depending on careful observations. It is relevant to ask, "In what sense, then, does structural analysis provide human information?" Recall that we defined human information as data and models. Both examples *are* models—but without empirical data. And they provide valuable information about social structures.

Note the enormous power and freedom that structural analysis provides. For instance, Arrow formulated his axioms to describe properties that intuitively seem "fair." But he was not bound by such intuitions—in fact, in the years since Arrow's theorem was proven, many investigators have changed one or more of the axioms and asked "What would be the consequence if a voting procedure had these properties?"

Suppose a committee consists of four members with one designated as chair. All four vote on motions; in case of a 2-2 tie, the chair makes the decision. According to the Banzhaf power index, we can determine the relative power of each committee member as follows:

1. Denote the committee members by A, B, C, and D and let C denote the chair.

2. List all winning coalitions:

   ABCD (the "grand coalition")
   AB<u>C</u>
   <u>ABD</u>
   A<u>C</u>D
   B<u>C</u>D
   <u>AC</u>
   <u>BC</u>
   <u>CD</u>

3. Mark the critical voters in each coalition. We have done this above by italicizing them.

4. Count the number of times each voter is critical and total these numbers:

   A: 2   C: 6
   B: 2   D: 2
   Total: 12

5. The relative power of each member is the proportion of times that voter is critical:

   A: 16.7%   C: 50%
   B: 16.7%   D: 16.7%

That is, in this situation, the chair has three times as much power as does any member of the committee. In fact, the chair holds 1/2 of the power and all the remaining members together hold the remaining 1/2. (If these ratios seem surprising, note that the only way the chair's will can be thwarted is if the other three committee members band together in opposition.)

Figure 4.1.

Consider a metaphor. On July 1, 1940, the Tacoma Narrows bridge outside Seattle opened; on November 7, it collapsed. On the day of its collapse, a wind was blowing up the Narrows. It caused the bridge to vibrate severely and during a few hours the bridge literally tore itself apart, at the loss of millions of dollars and great inconvenience to many people. Fortunately no human lives were lost. But the failure of the bridge was an expensive way to uncover a design flaw. Today mathematical models have improved to the point that repetition of the Tacoma Narrows disaster is unlikely.

Structural analysis provides a similar capability for social structures. Arrow's theorem, for instance, tells us that the search for a perfect voting method is a chimera and we needn't waste our time seeking it. Thus, it shows us that there are intrinsic limits to the social structures we can design; this is invaluable information.

Further examples of structural analysis, such as organizational charts and data flow diagrams, are found in business. They provide a means to describe existing structures and to examine alternate organizational structures for many different characteristics, such as balance in supervisory loads, inconsistent reporting patterns, duplication of effort, and provision of adequate checks and balances. Economics uses structural analysis a great deal in studying various assumptions about economic systems. In political science, one example of structural analysis is the study of voting methods, another is the theory of games. Game theory also is studied in sociology and economics.

Structural analysis provides substantial social benefits besides freedom of inquiry. One is the provision of a substantive basis for intersubjective agreement, namely rigorous mathematical proof.[10] Thus, today no one questions the truth of Arrow's theorem.[11] Another is that it provides for clarity of thought and expression—in fact, it forces them. Thus, for many practitioners, the main benefit of mathematizing is that mathematics demands precision and clarity resulting in clearer thinking.

Another closely related benefit is also important. Once an idea has been precisely formulated and a theorem proven, the assumptions made and arguments used are explicitly laid out for public scrutiny. Concepts are typically refined until a compact, clear, precise formulation is found; proofs are carefully examined for correctness and are often improved by making them shorter and clearer. Thus, the process is completely open, communication is strongly encouraged, and a high value is set on intersubjective agreement. In short, in terms of the *contextual* norms suggested in Chapter 1, the process of structural analysis fares very well.

But there are assumptions and values intrinsic to structural analysis (as with any application of mathematics).

■ A high value is placed on precise and explicit statement of all definitions and hypotheses; ambiguity must be avoided because it does not lend itself to mathematical analysis. To provide clarity and precision, complex concepts are simplified. For example, Banzhaf's index precisely defines a very limited concept of power—all dimensions of personal influence and legislative skills are ignored. With Banzhaf's index, this simplification is useful (as long as we remember that it is a simplification.) In Chapter 6, we shall see how this "precising" process can at times be harmful.

■   "Truth" is defined as logical consistency. Other important concepts of truth, such as correspondence to reality or truth-in-being (in such phrases as "He is a true friend") are not considered.

■   Simplicity is valued. Given two expressions of the same idea, the simpler is usually preferred because it lends itself more effectively to analysis. An alternative to Banzhaf's index is the Shapley-Shubik index, derived from n-person game theory.[12] The Shapley-Shubik index is defined in terms of when a member joins the coalition, not only on whether the member is critical. Banzhaf's index often is used only because it is simpler.

■   Generality is valued—that is, it is assumed that form can be separated from content with no essential loss of meaning. For instance, Banzhaf's index is used for county and for state legislatures and for legislatures of different sizes. It can be used in different cultures. No attention is paid to these contextual issues.

■   A high value is set on playfulness—on exploring alternate structures and investigating their ramifications simply for the sheer joy of creativity and discovery.

Thus, the investigator who chooses structural analysis as a mode of thinking will try to identify critical factors in a situation and to define them precisely. He or she will try to generalize by abstracting and separating the problem from its original context. He or she will play with ideas and possibilities, preferring simpler expressions of ideas to more complex ones if two expressions are otherwise equivalent. And the criterion of truthfulness will be logical consistency.

We now can see the limitations of structural analysis. In fact, its very strength is its limitation. The freedom it provides also limits its capabilities. Because the methodological constraints are the requirements of precision and clarity, logical consistency, simplicity, and generality, the method provides no restraint that prevents violation of contextual norms. For example, in Arrow's theorem, axiom 5 asserts the assumption that there is no dictator. But if this axiom is removed, it is easy to show that the decision function that simply makes one decision maker's preference list into the composite list will satisfy the other four axioms. There is nothing in the methodology that would say that such a decision function is inappropriate. As we pointed out in Chapter 1, problems are often encountered in medicine that are expressed as "We *can* do X but *should* we?" That is, principles and values from outside medicine itself are required to evaluate the appropriateness of some actions. The use of structural analysis is similar: Norms from outside mathematics itself are required to assess the appropriateness of assumptions. Another way of expressing this is that although structural analysis allows us to formulate many different possible structures and explore the properties of each, the technical values of simplicity and generality may be insufficient to decide which structure is "better."

Another limitation of structural analysis is that mathematics brings its own agenda. Economists, sociologists, or political scientists who engage in structural analysis find themselves in a world of existence and uniqueness theorems and a multitude of other technical issues that have little to do with the original question that motivated the analysis. And because structural analysis requires no empirical foundation, its freedom can lead to what some critics of mathematical social science regard as a profusion of rigorous mathematical nonsense. For instance, the mathematician John Von Neumann[13] warned that mathematics easily

> becomes more and more purely aestheticizing, more and more purely *l'art pour l'art*. This need not be bad, if the field is surrounded by correlated subjects, which have still closer empirical connections, or if the discipline is under the influence of men with an exceptionally well-developed taste. But there is a grave danger the subject will develop along the lines of least resistance, that the stream, so far from its source, will separate into a multitude of insignificant branches, and that the discipline will become a disorganized mass of details and complexities. In other words, a great distance from its empirical source, or after much "abstract" inbreeding, a mathematical subject is in danger of degeneration. At its inception the style in usually classical; when it shows signs of becoming baroque, then the danger signal is up. It would be easy to give examples, to trace specific evolutions into the baroque and the very high baroque. (p. 29)

A difficult trade-off arises at this point between the freedom mathematics provides to explore intriguing nuances and the more pragmatic goal of developing socially useful structures. There is no easy resolution to this dilemma because we never know in advance which discoveries are going to prove practically useful. So, individuals and granting agencies make the best guesses they can about how to invest their resources while trying not to discourage others with a different vision.

In summary, then, we have developed some principles that ought to guide the use of structural analysis in the social sciences: First, we need to regard it as a powerful and valuable tool that enables us to envision potential new social structures, to formulate them clearly, and to test them in an artificial setting before subjecting people to undiscovered flaws. Second, it does not lend itself to problems that cannot be formulated precisely or that cannot be separated from context. In fact, it can actually impoverish our understanding if we become so enamored with our precise, simplified representation that we forget the complexity of the original concept and context from which our mathematical formulation arose. And third, structures that violate contextual norms (such as compassion, stewardship, and respect for persons) may still be consistent, simple, and general; if structural analysis is to avoid violating contextual norms, its practitioners must continually consider such norms.

▧ NORMATIVE DECISION MAKING

As we pointed out earlier, the word "normative" in the phrase "normative decision making" does not have the same meaning as used elsewhere in this book. In decision science, it refers to *prescriptive* modeling of decisions (models designed to identify the "best" decision in a situation) as contrasted to *descriptive* models (that describe the process decision makers use). As an example of normative decision making, we have selected linear programming.

Linear programming is not a form of computer programming but is a mathematical model in which many decision problems can be formulated. For a simplified example, suppose the manager of a coal-fired electric power generating plant wants to maximize production of electricity, subject to some legal restrictions on air pollution and the limitations of its conveyor's and pulverizer's capacity. It can burn either hard and soft coal, each of which produces different amounts of heat and different amounts of pollutants. The manager must decide what quantities of hard and soft coal to use.[14]

We will show briefly how this problem can be formulated mathematically. First, the electricity is generated by steam and the amount of electricity produced is directly proportional to the amount of steam produced. Thus, the manager can focus on maximizing steam production. Steam production, however, is directly related to the amount and type of coal burned. Suppose 24 tons of steam are produced by each ton of hard coal burned and 20 tons of steam by each ton of soft coal. If we let x denote the number of tons of hard coal and y the number of tons of soft coal, we can state the manager's objective as

$$\text{maximize } (24x + 20y)$$

The legal and physical constraints can be formulated as inequalities. Suppose that each ton of hard coal produces 0.5 kg. of particle emissions (that is, smoke) and each ton of soft coal produces 1.0 kg. of particle emissions. If particle emissions are restricted by law to a maximum of 12 kg. per hour, then the smoke constraint can be expressed as

$$0.5x + 1.0y \leq 12$$

We will skip the details and simply note that the legal constraints on sulfur dioxide emissions and the limited capacities of the pulverizer and conveyor produce inequalities similar to the smoke inequality.

$$x + y \leq 20 \text{ (conveyor)}$$

$$(1/16)x + (1/24)y \leq 1 \text{ (pulverizer)}$$

$$1200x - 800y \geq 0 \text{ (sulfur dioxide)}$$

And finally, because we cannot burn negative quantities of either type of coal, we have the so-called nonnegativity constraints

$$x \geq 0$$

$$y \geq 0$$

See Figure 4.2 for a graphical representation of the "admissible solutions"—those values of x and y that satisfy the constraints. Linear program-

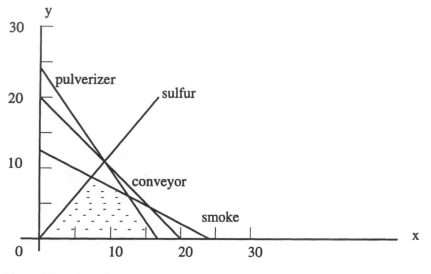

Figure 4.2.

ming provides mathematical methods for choosing the admissible solution that maximizes steam production.

Linear programming originated in military and transportation problems. It has since come to be used for a variety of decision problems, such as controlling the cracking of petroleum, selecting investment portfolios, optimizing factory productivity, planning survey distribution strategies, scheduling factory workers, mixing concrete, designing the product mix for a fruit processing plant, hauling dirt, and managing publishing schedules.

Normative decision making occupies an odd position in the use of empirical and mathematical methods—its usefulness depends on its capacity to model real world decisions and provide helpful advice. The models themselves are formulated (more or less) axiomatically and hence are similar to the formal mathematics used in structural analysis. But the models are intended to represent (a simplified) reality and hence their usefulness depends on the skill of the modeler in selecting the characteristics to be represented and representing them accurately. Furthermore, parameters in the models (such as the quantities of steam and smoke produced per ton of coal in our example) often need to be obtained empirically.

Normative decision making provides a means to make quite explicit the assumptions and values on which a decision is based. For instance, to use linear programming, one has to identify very clearly what the objective is—that is, what characteristic is to be maximized or minimized. (The method can be extended beyond our example to handle more than one objective.) In the choice of the objective, one's values are made explicit. One also has to identify what the decision variables are—that is, what aspects of the situation can be controlled. Typically the kinds of problems to which linear programming lends itself well are problems in the allocation of scarce resources. Thus, one has to model the scarcity constraints inherent in the situation. And to write equations, one has to understand how the numerical values of the decision variables become translated into numerical values of the objective. These are tall orders! But the entire model explicitly presents what is assumed about the constraints and the dynamics of how numerical values of the decision variables are transformed into corresponding numerical values of the objective. Once the assumptions are made this clear, they are open to critique by anyone who reviews the model. Linear programming also has been quite effective in solving many problems. For instance, enormous financial savings have been made in such processes as cracking petroleum and airline scheduling.

But linear programming is not the only technique used by practitioners of normative decision making. Other models (known as decision-theoretic models) allow for risk assessment. Also, there are models, such as PERT (Program Evaluation and Review Technique) and CPM (Critical Path Method), for scheduling activities like major construction projects, models from queuing theory for the management of waiting lines, and other models as well.

Now that we have sketched the concept of normative decision making and indicated some of its benefits, we turn to its underlying assumptions and values and how they can influence an investigator's thinking. We can build on the previous two sections. The assumptions and values of normative decision making are the composite of those from empirical methods and structural analysis, with (at least) one major addition: a high value is set on optimizing attainment of an objective.

As for the influence of these assumptions and values on the decision maker, linear programming has been so successful that it has proven to be a powerful example. Thus, the decision analyst with linear programming in mind perceives situations in terms of objective functions to be maximized or minimized, alternatives to be identified, and functions that transform these alternatives into numerical values of the objective function.

But normative decision making is a relatively young discipline; there are problems with it and significant critiques have been advanced. Its major exemplar, linear programming, was only developed in the late 1940s and early 1950s. First, its standards of persuasiveness are still somewhat fuzzy. By and large, the field of normative decision making has tended to become more like formal mathematics and less empirical. But some practitioners are calling for a strengthening of its empirical aspects.[15] Furthermore, much normative decision analysis is often done for clients and so is not open for public scrutiny. Peer review does not occur in these situations, and thus the standard of persuasiveness is the credibility of the analyst. In such situations the benefits that can be obtained by openness are lost.

Second, a major challenge to the primary exemplars of the discipline recently has been issued. Ralph Keeney has introduced an approach to decision analysis in which consideration of values is the starting point. In the introduction to his recent book, he wrote,

> Almost all of the literature on decision making concerns what to do *after* the crucial activities of identifying the decision problems, creating alternatives, and specifying objectives. But where do these decision problems, alternatives and objectives come from? This book describes and illustrates the creative processes that you should follow to identify your decision problems, create alternatives, and articulate your objectives. These prescriptions are quite different from the way people typically pursue these activities.[16] (Preface)

A third critique is related to Keeney's analysis. The tendency of a decision analyst is to look at a new situation through linear programming eyes and hence to seek objective functions to maximize, explicit decision variables to select values for, and constraints that affect those variables. But many situations, notably ones in which human relationships are the central dynamics, do not lend themselves well to this kind of analysis. The use of linear programming is very algorithmic—it is an archetypal example of Ellul's concept of technique discussed in Chapter 1. As such, it focuses on impersonal aspects of decisions—verifiable outcomes, quantifiable objectives, and so forth. Consequently, such personal qualities of leadership as compassion and reliability easily can be disregarded.

And fourth, several related critiques arise from normative decision-making mathematical formalization. Users tend to focus on factors that can be quantified. Factors that are not easily quantified tend to be ignored. Because the modeler formulates the objective function, it is easy for the modeler to impose his or her values on everyone affected by the decision.

Because the dynamics are often hard to identify, it is easy to adjust one's assumptions about those dynamics to produce a recommended decision that fits someone's preconceptions. And as more formal techniques are developed, researchers tend to become more and more specialized and lose perspective on the meaning and purposes of the entire process.

Finally, then, we can develop some principles that can guide in the use of normative decision making. First, data and models have indeed proven to be powerful tools in improving decision making in several areas, but they have significant limitations as well. As we have argued throughout this book, an understanding of such limitations is essential if we are to avoid doing harm. For instance, in linear programming, the objectives chosen could violate the contextual norms cited in Chapter 1—the technique for solving linear programming problems is mathematically as effective with unacceptable objectives as with acceptable objectives. Physical constraints may be inadvertently overlooked; ethical constraints may be deliberately neglected if doing so results in a larger value of the objective function. The dynamics may not be understood well enough to justify forming equations, but the method may be used anyway. The results still appear precise and so may be accorded a credibility they don't deserve. Second, the best means for addressing these limitations is openness. Nonexpert users of the results that decision analysts produce need to be made familiar with these limitations and encouraged to question the assumptions made in decision models. And modelers ought to submit their work for scrutiny by other professional modelers whenever possible.

Furthermore, everyone involved in the decision process needs to keep in mind that decision modeling and analysis are conducted in a context that involves human beings. The modeling and analysis should help decision makers make better decisions. But the context may subvert this outcome. For instance, financial incentives may distort the modeler's perception of the situation being modeled, or models that represent situations well may be rejected by whomever commissioned the model, or a common model may be used when it does not properly apply.

LIMITED OBJECTIVITY

Having completed our overview of the *a priori* influences on how the need for information is perceived and how questions are formulated, it is clear that the Cartesian hope of a value-free, presupposition-free, objective science is indeed unrealizable. But a limited notion of objectivity still is meaningful, we believe.

All observations are made by human beings who have purposes, prior understandings, and beliefs that affect what they perceive. If they are scientists, they use methods that themselves include assumptions and values that affect perception. But the purposes and background of the observation need not be hidden—they can be acknowledged and deliberate efforts made to counter their influence. Methods can be carefully scrutinized to see whether they apply in specific situations. In fact, the intrinsic values of science include an expectation that biasing influences be countered and the peer review process exists to assist in this process. Of course, if the entire scientific community shares a bias, this process will not uncover it. But science and mathematics operate very much like formal games in which precise rules have been carefully worked out and are explicitly laid out for public scrutiny. If such a bias should ever be discovered, the rules themselves require that, if possible, they be changed to remove it. And, although many specific examples of biased work have been found, no compelling evidence of a consistent bias has been forthcoming.

The perfect objectivity assumed by logical positivists is indeed not attainable, but it need not be rejected entirely. It can be approximated. Objectivity is as impossible as a perpetual motion machine or a perfectly fair voting method. But impossibility does not prevent us from making machines as efficient and voting methods as fair as possible. The notion of objectivity serves as a *regulative ideal*[17] that we continually strive to approximate more closely.

In summary, this book is about seeking normative principles that guide us toward the regulative ideal of objectivity; the next chapter continues our walk through the information cycle as we attempt to do this.

▓ NOTES

1. For example, see Kling and Iaconno (1988).
2. See Hock (1992, p. 69).
3. Note that theory construction often precedes observation. In fact, the theory often guides what is looked for and the questions asked. It may even influence what is observed.
4. For an extended discussion of this point, see Lieberson (1985).
5. See Skinner (1971).
6. See Rorty (1979).

7. There are many publications in which a mathematically more precise formulation can be found. For instance, see Arrow and Raynaud (1986).

8. For an excellent, thorough discussion of the five properties and the significance of Arrow's theorem, see MacKay (1980).

9. This index was first discussed in print in Banzhaf (1965). It also has been discussed in several other publications. For instance, see Brams, Lucas, and Straffin, Jr. (1983).

10. In fact, the concept of mathematical proof is not quite as objective as once was hoped—mathematicians never write out detailed step-by-step arguments in which every step can be justified by a well-established rule of inference. Rather, proofs are arguments that convince other mathematicians and that mathematicians believe can be converted into detailed step-by-step proofs (although no one ever does the conversion). Nevertheless, convincing proofs do provide a broad basis for agreement even by people who do not read the proof with care themselves but are willing to believe the mathematicians who have.

11. A proof can be found in Arrow and Raynaud (1986). It is less than two pages in length.

12. This also is discussed in Brams et al. (1983).

13. As quoted in Poundstone (1992).

14. From Daellenbach, George, and McNickle (1983).

15. For instance, see Meredith (1995).

16. See Keeney (1996).

17. See Phillips (1992).

Measurement of Human Information

THE SOCIAL UTILITY OF MEASUREMENT

Why is so much human data collected? One reason is that a good system of measurement provides substantial benefits. Consider a simple example that will lead us into several important concerns about the social and decision sciences. Because Ed Thompson's home has very hard well water, he has a water softener in his basement. To keep it operating properly, he must dump a bag of salt crystals into its tank every few weeks. His grocery store carries these in 40-pound bags and 80-pound bags. He has a weak back so he always buys the 40-pound bags; he cannot safely lift the 80-pound bags.

Now consider the same situation supposing there were no way to measure weight. One way Ed could judge how heavy a bag of crystals will feel to him is by its apparent size. But if he misjudges, he risks injuring his back. Alternatively, he could ask a clerk if a particular bag is light. But "light weight" to the clerk may not be "light weight" to him. (Also such requests could consume a lot of clerk time.) In fact, Ed has no means to predict whether or not a particular bag is safe for him to lift. Furthermore, the store manager has no means to select an equitable price for bags of salt. She has two choices.

1. Price all bags equally and have an employee fill each bag to an amount he judges to be about the same. Perhaps even small, medium, and large bags could be distinguished. But then customers may spend considerable time hefting bags and disturbing the display to get the most for their money. Also, complaints of the "Sam got more than I got for the same price" variety are inevitable.

2. Fill bags differently, but price each bag based on one employee's subjective estimate of heaviness. This might be close to consistent if one employee priced all the bags, but all of the same problems would likely arise.

This example illustrates several social benefits of measurement.

1. Measurement provides predictive power. Because Ed is familiar with 40-pound and 80-pound weights, he knows exactly how the two sizes of bags will affect his back without having to lift either.

2. Measurement enriches language by enabling us to transcend our individual subjective experiences. The fact that a clerk informs Ed that a bag of salt feels light to her does not tell Ed that it will feel light to him (unless he has heard her comment frequently on bags he has subsequently lifted). But if the clerk tells him an unmarked bag weighs 80 pounds, he knows exactly and immediately what that means for him without having to lift the bag himself. That is, he can learn from and make inferences based on the observations of others.

Measurement also enables us to resolve subjective disagreements about direct judgments ("This bag is heavy." "No, it's not.") and comparative judgments ("Bag A is heavier than bag B." "No, B is heavier."). And measurement allows us to make judgments about the observations of others. That is, if Laura consistently calls 40-pound bags "light," Ed has a clearer insight into Laura's subjective judgments of weight than he would if he only knew that Laura calls bags light that he calls heavy. Also, if Sam consistently underestimates weights, Ed can take this into account when hearing a weight estimated by Sam.

3. Measurement provides a framework for dealing with error. If Ed believes a bag weighs less than the 40 pounds he paid for but the store manager does not, they have a mutually agreeable means to identify

whether the bag was labeled erroneously. Such agreement is possible because they share a mutual belief that there is a unique single value, which is the weight of the bag. Differences in measurement then are attributable to measurement error not to differences in values, perceptions, frames of reference, or dishonesty.

4. Measurement enhances one form of social justice, namely equity. Among the many notions of justice, one notion is "fairness"—treating everyone the same. Measurement is a means of implementing fairness— everyone pays the same price for the same 40-pound bag of salt independent of age, gender, religion, race, or any other characteristic. There are, of course, situations in which equity is not fair—for example, a person born with a physical disability should not be treated identically as a person born without a physical disability. But the use of measurement to provide fairness eliminates many opportunities for preferential or discriminatory treatment that is unjust by any reasonable standard. In fact, the classical image of justice is a blindfolded woman holding a balance scale. That is, measurement of weight is a metaphor for justice in any area.

5. Measurement provides an incentive for the accumulation of knowledge. Confidence in the truthfulness of information is an important (perhaps essential) incentive for believing that information. A good system of measurement provides confidence that information is being reported truthfully. Once information is trusted, further data and information can be built on it.

6. Measurement enables us to make finer distinctions than we can make with ordinary language. Consider the measurement of temperature. Imagine a parent who calls a doctor because his child has a fever. If he says, "My child feels warm," the doctor has little basis on which to recommend action. But if he is able to report the child's temperature, the doctor does have such a basis—a temperature of 40°C (104°F) is a cause for serious concern, whereas a temperature of 38°C (100.4°F) signifies a mild fever. But on the Kelvin scale (on which temperature is proportional to the amount of heat present, unlike the Celsius and Fahrenheit scales), the difference between 40°C and 38°C is only 0.65%, a relatively small difference. Yet such a small difference gives the doctor a great deal of helpful insight.

In summary, then, enormous social benefits are derivable from systems of measurement that become widely accepted. This is why "measurement" is such an important topic to consider before practicing the social and decision sciences. To the extent that measurement in these fields is muted or impossible, researchers and practitioners will experience difficulty predicting, transcending their subjective impressions, learning or making inferences from others' observations, considering and dealing with error, promoting justice, accumulating knowledge, and making fine distinctions. In short, their work will be severely hampered.

Furthermore, in this book we are trying to develop principles that can guide the collection and use of human information. The source of such information is often a measurement. Thus, we cannot lay a foundation for assessing the collection and use of human information without carefully examining measurement.[1]

▓ WHAT ENABLES MEASUREMENT?

What principles should guide attempts to measure human qualities if we are to obtain the benefits that measurement can provide? As we have seen, in order to discover methodological norms, we must carefully assess the technical issues involved, inasmuch as many methodological norms are determined by the capabilities and limitations of the technical methods. Thus we begin by clarifying what makes measurement possible.[2] Unfortunately, this section is somewhat technical; nevertheless, there is no way to come to an understanding of the capabilities and limitations of measurement without working through this technical material.

Four requirements for measurement are

1. a precise, unambiguous definition of the characteristic being measured;
2. an interpersonal consensus on ranking, relative to the characteristic;[3]
3. a set of theoretical properties of the measurement of the characteristic on which a broad consensus is attainable; and
4. a technique of measurement that is consistent with the definition, the ranking, and the theoretical properties.

Our first principle is that measurement techniques need to meet these requirements. These require some explanation and some justification.[4] To begin, we need to talk about different types of measurement scales. As we do so, the need for the four requirements just mentioned will become clear.

Most measurements with which we are familiar (such as weight, time, length, and temperature) are numerical. But, in fact, not all measurement

TABLE 5.1 Some Types of Measurement Scales

Type	Example	Measurement-Preserving Transformations
Nominal	Numbering of uniforms Telephone numbers	Any one-to-one function
Ordinal	Rankings of college football teams Air quality Student letter grades	Any monotonic increasing function $[x \geq y$ if and only if $f(x) \geq f(y)]$
Interval	Temperature (Fahrenheit or Celsius) Calendar time Cardinal utility	Any positive linear transformation $[f(x) = ax+b$ where $a > 0]$
Ratio	Temperature (Kelvin) Mass Length Time intervals	Any similarity transformation $[f(x) = ax$ where $a > 0]$
Absolute	Counting Probability	Only the identity transformation $[f(x) = x]$

needs to be done on the real numbers. We list five commonly used types of scales in Table 5.1 from the least structured to the most structured. Note that the most structured scales are also the most familiar to us and thus may *seem* simpler (which opens the door to their misuse). Also note that one column of Table 5.1 is headed "Measurement-preserving transformations." We will discuss this notion later in this section after we have discussed the five data types.

Nominal (or *categorical*) scales need not involve numbers and could be regarded as simply providing categories, not measurements (if one wanted to insist that measurements must be numerical). But because categories can be numbered, it is simpler to think of nominal scales as providing a measurement. Thus, such data as gender, city of residence, and type of automobile are examples of nominal data. Numbers on athletic uniforms are a familiar example of numbers used to denote nominal data—the fact that one number is larger than another usually means nothing. Telephone numbers are another example.

Ordinal scales provide only a ranking—first to last, highest to lowest, and so forth. Some examples are the rankings of Olympic divers by judges and a list of ice cream flavors ranked by an individual from most preferred

TABLE 5.2 Requirements of the Five Common Scales

	Unambiguous Definition	Interpersonal Agreement on Rankings	Two Fixed Points and Linearity	True Zero Plus One Fixed Point	No Arbitrary Values
nominal	*				
ordinal	*	*			
interval	*	*	*		
ratio	*	*	*	*	
absolute	*	*	*	*	*

to least preferred. Ordinal scales cannot tell us how much more (or less) of a factor one item has than another. That is, an ordinal scale can tell us that a first-place diver performed better in the judges' assessment than a third-place diver. But it cannot tell us that the first-place diver outperformed the third-place diver by the same amount that the third-place diver outperformed the fifth-place diver.

The archetypal example of an *interval* scale is temperature in degrees Fahrenheit or Celsius. On interval scales, subtraction and addition are meaningful, but multiplication and division are not. That is, a statement as "After she took her medicine, Suzy's temperature dropped one degree" is meaningful regardless of whether her temperature was initially 38°C or 40°C. But 20°C is not twice as hot as 10°C because 0°C does not mean absence of heat—it is simply the temperature at which water freezes.

On *ratio* scales, multiplication and division are also meaningful. Eighty pounds is indeed twice as heavy as 40 pounds, because zero pounds truly means no weight. (That is, two 40-pound objects can be combined into a single 80-pound object.) But the non-zero numbers used are in no sense absolute—40 pounds is the same as 18.2 kilograms. In fact, any weight in pounds can be divided by 2.2 to get the corresponding weight in kilograms. Many other scales for weight are possible and familiar—grams, tons, ounces, stones—depending on what one selects as one unit of weight.

A typical example of an *absolute* scale is a count, for instance, the number of people in a room. Absolute scales do not allow for changes in scale because they are not measured relative to a unit. All arithmetic operations are meaningful and no scaling can be done without changing meaning. See Table 5.2 for a summary of the increasing structure associated with the scales.

To see why this hierarchy of scales is important for understanding human information, imagine someone attempting to develop a new measurement of some characteristic, a problem social scientists frequently face. For instance, suppose a psychologist wants to develop a numerical measure of the intensity of a human emotion, such as hostility. (We will critique an actual attempt to measure human stress at the end of Chapter 6.) Measurement theorists faced with a problem like this tend to start with the least structured scale, the nominal scale, and see how much structure can be added. Thus, the first question our psychologist must ask is "Can I define hostility clearly?" The definition of hostility could be a collection of clearly described states characterized in some way—perhaps by external behavior or some form of neurological activity. The second question that must be asked is "Can I tell when two states represent the same level of hostility?" States having the same level are collected together into "equivalence classes"— that is, collections of states all of which have equal amounts of hostility.[5]

If hostility cannot be defined clearly enough to identify equivalence classes, an alternate approach might be to abandon the attempt to measure hostility itself and introduce a "proxy"—a measurable entity that is believed to be closely related to hostility. We will discuss proxies more in Chapter 6, but for now let's suppose our psychologist has succeeded in defining hostility and identifying several equivalence classes, so a proxy is not needed. For numerical measurement in which the numbers serve as more than mere labels of categories, our psychologist needs to be able to distinguish which of two classes contains states that represent more hostility than the other. In fact, for such a measure to be socially useful there must be broad agreement on which represents more. Thus, if the equivalence classes can be ranked in some meaningful and broadly acceptable way, an ordinal scale applies. Now suppose that there is no true zero (i.e., no way to identify complete absence of hostility). Suppose also that two clearly identifiable standards for comparison can be selected (analogous to the boiling and freezing temperatures for water). Our psychologist can award these standards arbitrary values and an interval scale *potentially* can be established. (More is needed, as we shall shortly see.) If there is a true zero (a class of states whose members have a complete absence of hostility), one class can be selected as a standard for comparison, used as the unit, and then a ratio scale *may* be established.

We now can see why the four requirements are needed for measurement. Consider first clear definition. Without a clear definition of hostility, it is impossible to precisely delineate equivalence classes, and hence we can't even get to first base—namely a nominal scale.[6] Put differently, unless we have an unambiguous way (apart from the arbitrary assignment of the same numerical value) to tell when two states represent exactly the same amount of hostility, measurement is meaningless.

To add more structure than is contained in a nominal scale, however, requires interpersonal agreement on a ranking of the classes. Measurement can enable us to transcend individual subjective experience, but if there is no intuitive interpersonal agreement on ranking, there is no basis to move beyond subjectivity. With such an agreement, however, we are assured of at least an ordinal scale. Note that this agreement need not be one that all humanity would accept. If a group of scholars or practitioners agree on a ranking, they may choose to disregard those who disagree. Thus, a particular professional community may agree on a ranking that other professional communities may reject. That community can proceed to form its own measure.[7] Also, a researcher may come forward and advocate a ranking that no one else will accept initially. Subsequently some scholars, practitioners, or both may come to see the wisdom in it. For those who are persuaded, an ordinal scale (at least) is achievable.

Recall that the third requirement for measurement was a broadly acceptable theory of the characteristic. We will use ratio scales to explain this assertion. The development of a ratio scale for human hostility is not as simple as identifying a true zero and a unit, although these need to be done. The fact that one can identify a true zero and a unit provides no guarantee that there is any meaningful correspondence between the value of the characteristic at numerical values other than 0 and 1. For instance, there is no reason to believe that the state that measures 0.5 is "halfway between" the states that measure 0 and 1 in any meaningful sense. The establishment of such a correspondence requires a theory of hostility.

Let's leave hostility for a moment and consider something simpler to measure, namely weight. Empirically, we know that combining two bags of flour gives the same numerical values for weight as adding the weights of the two separate bags. We can formalize this observation as an axiom:

$$w(a+b) = w(a) + w(b)$$

where a and b represent two objects, $a+b$ represents their combination, $w(a)$ represents a's weight, $w(b)$ represents b's weight, and $w(a) + w(b)$ represents the arithmetic sum of the two weights. When developing a measure for a characteristic, a measurement theorist typically studies the measurement of the characteristic empirically until a set of its properties can be formally articulated as a set of axioms. Then a "representation theorem" is proven; typically this takes the form of a mathematical proof that the set of axioms formulated is sufficient to establish a meaningful correspondence between the characteristic and the real numbers. Thus, in the case of weight, this means that there is a direct correspondence[8] between the act of combining weights and the mathematical operation of addition.

It is typically the case that one's observations, when formulated as axioms, don't immediately lend themselves to the proof of a representation theorem. A certain amount of interaction between theory and observation takes place at this point. The theorist looks at the axioms initially formulated and sees what additional axioms are needed to make the proof of a representation theorem possible. The theorist then returns to the characteristic at hand and checks whether the axioms needed correspond to actual properties of the characteristic that were not previously observed.

If a representation theorem can be proven, the next step is to prove a uniqueness theorem. This means identifying the class of changes that are allowed in the measure without destroying its underlying meaning. Thus with weight, if an object has weight x on some scale, any other scale that gives it weight ax, where $a > 0$, is still an acceptable measure of weight. Note that means that the zero value is preserved, but the former unit (which had value 1) is changed to a new value, a. The value of a cannot be negative because that would reverse the ranking; it cannot be zero because that would result in all objects having the same measure. With temperature, if a body has temperature T, any other scale that gives it value $aT + b$, where $a > 0$ and b is any real number, is still an acceptable measure of temperature. In this case, the zero is not preserved, but the relative sizes of differences are preserved. These transformations are the "measurement-preserving transformations" of Table 5.1.

Returning to our example of human hostility, to justify using an interval or ratio scale to measure hostility, one must be able to identify underlying properties of hostility that demonstrate that hostility behaves in the same way that numbers behave. This is why we said earlier that an interval scale *potentially* can be established when two fixed points can be identified. We saw earlier that for weight this means observing properties, such as the property that the weight of combined objects is the sum of their individual weights. The less structured nominal and ordinal scales do not require as extensive a theory, but they are not theory-free either. A nominal scale requires a precise enough definition of hostility that equivalence classes are well-defined; an ordinal scale requires a strictly hierarchical ranking of the equivalence classes that is mutually agreeable to the community that will use the measure.

And last, some "instrument" is needed to implement the measure. An instrument is a standard of comparison, typically with some equivalence categories indicated. Thus a meter stick is an instrument and the markings on it indicate the equivalence classes for length. Likewise an unambiguous survey question with a Likert scale (strongly agree, agree, neutral, disagree, strongly disagree) is an instrument and the five possible responses denote the equivalence classes. Ideally an instrument needs to yield the same measurement no matter who uses it. Some room for measurement error is allowed, however, as long as the measurement process has a sufficiently well-established theory to guarantee that measurements are unique. If it is to be socially useful, the technique must yield measurements that agree with broadly held intuitions about the characteristic in question. For instance, for an ordinal scale like the Likert scale, the measurements it yields are the responses "strongly agree, agree, neutral, disagree, strongly disagree." Regardless of the question asked, everyone intuitively agrees that "strongly agree" is a more positive response than "agree," that "agree" is more positive than "neutral," and so forth. The technique also must be demonstrably consistent with the theoretical properties of the measurement of the quantity. Some of the difficulties in meeting these standards are explored in Chapter 6.

The perspective we have presented here is based on measurement theory. There is an alternate point of view that holds that measurements do not need to be grounded in carefully established theories but are simply social conventions that aid communication. Such a perspective is widely held in psychometrics.[9] We do not agree—it seems to us that such an approach undermines the social benefits of measurement we cited in the previous section, and we regard these benefits as too valuable to sacrifice.

MEASUREMENT IN
THE SOCIAL SCIENCES

At this point, it is easy to see why normative principles of measurement in the social sciences are needed. The social benefits of a good system of measurement are enormous. But the requirements for the development of such a system are stringent and not well understood. Thus, the temptation to cut corners is high. In fact, corner cutting may not be maliciously intended; it may simply represent ignorance of the requirements. Even so, poor measurement has the potential for considerable social harm, as we shall see in the next chapter.

Given the stringent requirements that must be met before measurement is possible, is it reasonable to expect that the benefits of measurement can be obtained in the social sciences? One conventional answer is "no." For instance, statements such as "Measurement is legitimate in the natural sciences, but human qualities are not measurable" are common, especially from people who have been strongly influenced by postmodern critiques of science. Nevertheless, we do not see any grounds for a broadly based rejection of measurement in the social sciences, although we recognize that such measurement is often difficult and, in some cases, impossible. In fact, because the potential benefits are so great, we believe that the pursuit of measurement in the social sciences is essential and that those who would steer the social sciences away from it risk depriving the human community of substantial benefits.

In this section, we will demonstrate that measurement in the social sciences can be meaningful and helpful by giving several examples of good measures, showing how they satisfy the requirements, and showing how they provide social benefits. In the next chapter, we will explore the limitations of measurement in the social sciences and conclude with some case studies.

Our first example involves blood alcohol levels. Blood alcohol level is a proxy for drunkenness. That is, the measurement of blood alcohol was motivated by the loss of lives and property resulting from drunk driving. But "drunkenness" is hard to define and in the absence of a clear definition, intersubjective agreement on when someone is "drunk" is all but impossible to obtain (particularly from the person who has consumed too much alcohol). Nevertheless, blood alcohol level can be defined precisely and has the critical property that higher blood alcohol levels are intuitively associated with greater degrees of drunkenness. Thus, by using blood alcohol level as a proxy for drunkenness, society gains a measure that provides all of the benefits listed at the beginning of the chapter. Of course, different individuals may respond to different levels of blood alcohol differently. Thus, society takes a risk in using this proxy—that persons whose judgment and driving skill are severely impaired by low blood alcohol levels are not socially regarded as drunk and may not even regard themselves as drunk. Still, the benefits of using the proxy seem to outweigh this risk.

Blood alcohol level is measured as a percentage, for example .08%, meaning .08 cc. of alcohol per 100 cc. of blood. Volume measures use ratio scales, but because alcohol level is a percentage, it is not dependent on the unit of measure and is, in fact, an absolute scale. Thus, phrases such as "a .08 level is twice as great as a .04 level" are meaningful. Such measurement has provided an unambiguous, legally enforceable definition of drunk driving, typically at a blood alcohol level greater than 0.10%.[10] The social benefits of blood alcohol measurement are clear; consider the five benefits we listed at the beginning of the chapter.

1. Measurement of blood alcohol has enabled us to predict when a driver is likely to be impaired.
2. Intersubjective disagreements of the form "You were driving drunk" "No, I wasn't drunk—I can hold my liquor" have been limited.
3. Justice (in the sense of equity of treatment) is enhanced because every driver is judged by the same standard.
4. The measurement of blood alcohol level has provided a strong incentive for further research on the effect of alcohol on driving.
5. Fine distinctions, such as between .06% and .08% blood alcohol, can be made.

The one benefit not fully realized is a framework for dealing with error, particularly important in a situation when lives and reputations are at stake. That is, a breathalyzer provides an indirect measure that is not perfectly correlated with blood alcohol. This is why new and more accurate techniques that use small blood samples are being developed.

It should be clear at this point that measurement in the social sciences is not only possible but has the potential to be extremely beneficial. But let's consider a few more examples.

Perhaps the most formative work in the history of sociology was Emile Durkheim's study of suicide in mid-19th century Europe, discussed briefly in Chapter 4. Durkheim approached the study of suicide through the use of suicide rates in different countries. (See Table 5.3.)[11]

Note that the measure Durkheim used—relative frequency—is an absolute measure, because it is based on counting. Thus, the data type is nonproblematic and enables the use of all common arithmetic operations; nevertheless, it is inevitable in the use of frequencies in this manner that

TABLE 5.3 Durkheim's Data on Suicides

Country	Insane Per 100,000	Suicide Per 100,000	Rank Order of Countries	
			Insanity	Alcoholism
Norway	180 (1855)	107 (1851-55)	1	4
Scotland	164 (1855)	34 (1856-60)	2	8
Denmark	125 (1847)	258 (1846-50)	3	1
Hannover	103 (1856)	13 (1856-60)	4	9
France	99 (1856)	100 (1851-55)	5	5
Belgium	92 (1858)	50 (1855-60)	6	7
Wurtemburg	92 (1853)	108 (1846-56)	7	3
Saxony	57 (1858)	245 (1856-60)	8	2
Bavaria	57 (1858)	73 (1846-56)	9	6

the measuring technique will have some problems in that records are not perfect, and classification of a death as a suicide may be difficult. Despite these potential difficulties, Durkheim found a surprising constancy in the suicide rate in each country from one year to the next. He wanted to explain why this constancy occurred and why the rates differed so much from country to country. He was quickly able to dismiss the hypothesis that it simply reflected different ways of recording the data. He examined many variables, including insanity and alcoholism rates. Whereas Durkheim did not have the statistical tools we have today, he observed (as we can easily do in Table 5.3) that there was little relationship between suicide and the reported insanity rate. Although it appears from Table 5.3 that there is a relationship between suicide and alcoholism, additional study did not support the existence of such a relationship. He also examined many traits of individuals as possible explanatory variables and finally abandoned the effort as unfruitful. He did observe, however, that the suicide rate was much higher in Protestant countries than Catholic countries and that this observation even held when Protestant and Catholic provinces within the same country were compared. (See Table 5.4.)

Durkheim could find no doctrinal differences between Protestantism and Catholicism that could account for this difference in suicide rate. Instead, he examined what he regarded as "the only essential difference"— that Protestants (at least at that time) permitted a much greater freedom of personal inquiry than did Catholics. Thus, Durkheim proposed that the greater the sense of community a religion provided, the less its suicide rate

TABLE 5.4 Comparison of Suicide Rates by Religious Persuasion

Religious Persuasion	Average Suicides Per Year Per 1 Million Inhabitants
Protestant	190
Mixed Protestant and Catholic	96
Catholic	58
Greek Catholic	40

would be. He hypothesized a variable he called "social integration" as the causative variable and predicted that people who lived in families would have much lower suicide rates than people who were single. He then collected substantial data to test this hypothesis and found significantly larger suicide rates among single than among married people, thus concluding that he had verified his hypothesis.

The social benefit of Durkheim's work was not the formulation of civil laws as was our previous example. Rather, it provided an understanding of a complex and troubling social phenomenon. (We shall see in Chapter 9 how such understandings play a critical role in the formation of public policy.) But note how Durkheim's work depended on having a nonproblematic measurement scale: The use of relative frequency provided for intersubjective agreement—everyone understands rates the same way. Also relative frequency gave Durkheim a tool to make meaningful comparisons between countries, and it gave his work sufficient credibility that it became an enormous incentive for the development of the discipline of sociology.

Next we consider items from the ACE (American Council on Education) survey developed by Alexander Astin of UCLA. The scale is used to measure demographic data, attitudes, values, and personal and political concerns of millions of students entering American colleges and universities each year. It is also used to make comparisons between students in different years and students at different colleges. Some typical items from the survey are given in Figure 5.1.

We can use the four requirements for measurement to assess the questions used in this survey. Note that the data collected are not numerical; they are either categorical (for example, gender) or ordinal (for example, "frequently, occasionally, not at all"). The authors of the survey have shown wisdom here. They have recognized that the properties of the characteristics they want to measure are not quantitative, so they have not labelled their categories with numbers. Categorical data only require clear

1. Your gender: Male   Female

. . .

22. Current religious preference: (Mark *one* in each column)

	Yours	Father's	Mother's
Baptist	Y	F	M
Eastern Orthodox	Y	F	M
Islamic	Y	F	M

. . .

24. For the activities below, indicate which ones you did *during the past year* (Mark *one* for each item)

	Frequently	Occasionally	Not at all
Attended a religious service	F	O	N
Was bored in class	F	O	N
Drank beer	F	O	N
Discussed politics	F	O	N

. . .

36. Indicate the importance to you personally of each of the following: (Mark *one* for each item)

	Essential	Very Important	Somewhat Important	Not Important
Becoming an authority in my field	E	V	S	N
Raising a family	E	V	S	N
Becoming a community leader	E	V	S	N

. . .

Figure 5.1. Sample questions from the ACE survey

definition—for example, gender and current religious preference. The use of ordinal data adds a further requirement—intersubjective agreement on a ranking of the categories. But again, the categories selected for these questions are relatively nonproblematic, although there may be some differences in interpretation of the categories "frequently," "occasionally," and "not at all." Another possible source of error is that the survey asks for self-reported data and people do misreport data for various reasons. We will say more about this in Chapter 6. But, with the exception of these two possible problems, the survey is sound and beneficial.

Now consider a fourth example: social class. A social class can be defined as a set of people who have been grouped together, based on common characteristics. Defined in this way, social class is based on the mathematical notion of a set—a well-defined and well-understood concept. As long as the common characteristics have been well-defined, social class becomes an unambiguous nominal scale; if a broadly accepted hierarchy is added, it becomes an ordinal scale.

The problem, however, has been the appropriate selection of the common characteristics. Various characteristics have been used, such as ownership or nonownership of capital, similar amounts of income and wealth, prestige, education, subculture, political power, and combinations of these. The usefulness of the concept has been reduced because of the confusion resulting from the lack of clear definition. Yet it remains the single most powerful explanatory concept in the field of sociology. It has predictive power in such factors as mortality rates, educational and occupational success, mental illness rates, life satisfaction, marriage patterns, and other factors. It certainly has been a critical concept in many social justice arguments, although its utility as an aid in achieving justice has been reduced by its lack of clear definition. The concept of social class illustrates an important point—to realize the benefits that measurement is capable of providing, the requirements need to be met. Nevertheless, even when they are not fully met, partial benefits still may be realized.

In our sequence of examples here, we have moved from two examples that used numerical data, to one that used both ordinal and categorical data, and finally, to one that involved strictly categorical data. But these are not the only possible measurement scales. One common problem that occurs with measurement in the social sciences is that practitioners who are not knowledgeable about measurement theory choose a measurement scale because it is familiar, even though there may not be an adequate theoretical foundation to justify use of that scale. We will see an example of this in the case study of stress at the end of Chapter 6. Thus, we conclude this section with an example in which the appropriate measurement scale is one that is relatively unfamiliar—a lattice—a nonnumerical scale that has more structure than a categorical scale but less than an ordinal scale.

One decision-making problem that has been widely studied in the past few years is the "stable marriage problem." In this problem, a collection of n single men and n single women each want to marry and must select a partner from among the n members of the opposite gender present in the problem. Each man has a ranking of the n women and each woman has a ranking of the n men. The problem is to find the "best" match. The stable marriage problem is a model for various real world problems and, with

TABLE 5.5 An Instance of the Stable Marriage Problem

Man	Preference Ranking of Men	Woman	Preference Ranking of Women
1	57126843	1	53761284
2	23754186	2	86357214
3	85146237	3	15624873
4	32741685	4	87324156
5	72513684	5	64738125
6	16758423	6	28534671
7	25763481	7	75218643
8	38457261	8	74152368

slight modification, is currently used to assign medical students to hospitals for their residency. It also could be used to assign trainees to jobs.

Table 5.5 presents an instance of a stable marriage problem with 8 men and 8 women. The lists to the right of each man and each woman present their preference ranking of the other gender; for instance, man 1's first choice is woman 5, his second choice is woman 7, and so forth. One characteristic that seems essential for an optimal solution is that a matching be "stable"—that is, there must be no two people in any group who prefer each other to the spouse to whom they are assigned. For instance, the following matching of men and women is unstable:

(15, 23, 38, 46, 57, 61, 74, 82).

Note that man 8 is matched with woman 2 but prefers woman 4. Similarly woman 4 is matched with man 7 but prefers man 8. Thus the matching is

TABLE 5.6 The Stable Matches for the Example of Table 5.5

M_0	(15, 23, 38, 46, 57, 61, 72, 84)
M_1	(18, 23, 35, 46, 57, 61, 72, 84)
M_2	(13, 26, 35, 48, 57, 61, 72, 84)
M_3	(18, 23, 31, 46, 57, 65, 72, 84)
M_4	(13, 26, 31, 48, 57, 65, 72, 84)
M_5	(18, 23, 31, 46, 52, 65, 77, 84)
M_6	(13, 26, 31, 48, 52, 65, 77, 84)
M_7	(13, 26, 32, 48, 51, 65, 77, 84)

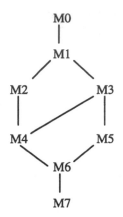

Figure 5.2. The lattice of stable matchings.

unstable because both man 8 and woman 4 can improve their situation by leaving their assigned spouse and joining with each other. Table 5.6 lists all of the stable matches.[12]

Researchers have shown that the collection of all stable matches can always be organized into a lattice.[13] (See Figure 5.2.) The match at the top is always "male optimal"—that is, in this match *every* man is assigned the most desirable partner he could have in any stable match. But the male optimal match is also "female pessimal"—*every* woman always receives the least desirable partner she could receive in any stable match. The bottom match is similarly "female optimal." As one traces a path from top to bottom, each match is successively less desirable to the men and more desirable to the women.

The lattice of stable matches can be regarded as a measurement scale in that it meets the requirements of a nominal scale—clearly defined categories. It has more structure than a nominal scale but less than an ordinal scale in the sense that on an ordinal scale, all elements are comparable, but on a lattice scale some are comparable (such as M0 and M1 inasmuch as all males prefer M0 to M1) but some are not (such as M2 and M3, inasmuch as some males prefer M2 and some prefer M3). Note how different this lattice is from a numerical scale—besides the fact that some elements are not comparable, which element is maximal and which element is minimal depends on whether one looks from the male or female perspective. Also, no arithmetic is incorporated in the structure, so there are no means, medians, or even totals.

Thus, the stable marriage problem illustrates a phenomenon we expect to see more of in the near future—the use of nontraditional, nonnumerical measurement scales in the social and decision sciences. Such an increase is likely because many human characteristics seem to lack the theoretical properties needed to justify numerical scales. But one need not respond to this lack by rejecting measurement entirely; rather, more appropriate scales need to be used.

In summary, then, we cannot find any coherent principle on which one could base a general rejection of measurement of human qualities, whether of individuals, groups, or human institutions. Nevertheless, because the requirements for meaningful measure are stringent, such measurement is often difficult and the numerical scales that are often used may not be appropriate. In Chapter 6 we explore some of the consequences of inappropriate measurement. We also examine the norms dictated by the limitations of measurement when gathering human information.

▓ NOTES

1. We are indebted to Henry Kyberg for many of the ideas in this chapter.

2. For readers interested in pursuing measurement theory in greater depth, we recommend three works. A fine elementary introduction is Chapter 7 of Olinick (1978). A thorough but readable advanced work is the three-volume study by Krantz, Luce, Suppes, and Tversky (1971); Suppes, Krantz, Luce, and Tversky (1989); and Luce, Krantz, Suppes, and Tversky (1990). For a treatment of measurement from a philosophical point of view, Kyberg (1984) is outstanding.

3. There appears to be a logical circularity here. In the first section of Chapter 5, we pointed out that one of the benefits of measurement is that it provides for intersubjective agreement. Now it seems that intersubjective agreement must exist before measurement is possible. In practice, when a new measure is being developed, preexisting intuitive agreements (which may be very vague) are used as a starting point. As the measure is developed, it is continually checked to see if it conforms to and/or enhances those intuitions. When fully developed, the measure enriches and strengthens the intuitive agreement that existed beforehand. It also provides consistency in application of the now-developed intuition.

4. We shall see in Chapter 6 that the list is redundant. Nevertheless, this redundancy need not concern us at this point.

5. If all the states represent different degrees of hostility, then each equivalence class consists of only one state.

6. In practice, however, the process of defining cannot be separated from the measurement technique used and the theoretical properties we identify for the characteristic. We will return to this point in some detail in the next chapter.

7. There are dangers in doing this. A community may be neglecting legitimate reasons that those outside the community may have for rejecting a measure. The point here is that the mathematics is meaningful. Whether its use in a situation is wise or expedient is another question entirely.

8. The mathematical name for such a correspondence is a "homomorphism"—literally meaning "of the same shape or same form."

9. For example, see Nunnally (1978).

10. Some American states are lowering the critical level to .08%.

11. This table and Table 5.2 are from Arney (1990).

12. This example is from Gusfield and Irving (1989, pp. 68-71).

13. A lattice is a partial order (that is, for some elements a strict preference order can be established, and for some no ranking can be established) in which there is one unique element that is preferred to all others and one other unique element to which all elements are preferred.

Limitations of
Measurement in
the Social Sciences

In Chapter 5 we discussed the potential benefits that can be derived from a system of measurement. We also discussed the requirements a measurement must meet to provide these benefits and showed several examples of effective measurements. This chapter begins by examining the dark side of measurement. We will parallel our discussion of benefits from good measurement with a discussion of possible harm from mismeasurement. We follow this with a reexamination of the four requirements for measurement to see what limitations they place on us in collecting human information if we are to avoid such harm. This leads to a statement of several contextual norms. And we will conclude with several case studies, including a brief evaluation of the most controversial human measurement in our times—the measurement of intelligence.

POSSIBLE SOCIAL HARMS
FROM MISMEASUREMENT

The first benefit discussed in Chapter 5 was predictive power. If Ed Thompson, our friend from the beginning of Chapter 5 with the weak back, sees a bag of salt labeled 40 pounds, he will feel safe in lifting it. But if the bag actually is a mislabeled 80-pound bag, he may injure himself. Incorrect or misleading measurements will result in wrong predictions. The consequences of such measurements can range from simple embarrassment to major harm.

For instance, standardized tests are often used to predict the potential academic success of young people. If such a test is inaccurate or misleading, a young person's ability to develop his or her gifts may be severely limited and society as a whole may be deprived of that person's contribution. Alternatively, suppose a charitable organization receives many proposals for projects and must select a relatively small number for funding. It develops a measurement scheme that enables it to compare projects. The purpose of such a measure is clearly predictive—to identify those projects that are going to bring the most benefit for the investment made in them. But if the measure is inadequate, poor selections may be made.

Our second benefit was that measurement enables us to transcend our subjectivity. But a misleading or inappropriate measure can fool us; it may result in misplaced and inappropriate decisions. Oftentimes these negative outcomes result from the illusion of precision and objectivity that a numerical measure provides.

For instance, an economic development organization may measure income production and use it as a basis for decision making, while ignoring social disruption. Alternatively, suppose a prominent ingredient in some common food, A, is believed to be dangerous. Large numbers of people may choose to replace item A in their diet with item B, which has less of the ingredient. But item B may have another ingredient that subsequently is discovered to be equally dangerous. That is, "dangerous" has been inappropriately measured. As a third example, executives in a company may make decisions based on the "bottom line" while paying insufficient attention to other matters that are also critical to its success, such as employee and customer satisfaction and good will. The executives have mismeasured "success." In each of these three cases, a precise, unambiguous, measurement—income produced, quantity of an ingredient, profit—was used as a proxy for a more general, more ambiguous concept—well-being, danger, or success. But it mismeasured the more general concept and thereby contributed to a potential for harm.

Poor measurement can lead to an impoverishment of understanding. If I learn that Billy's IQ score is higher than Bobby's, I may come away from that "learning experience" knowing less about Billy and Bobby than I did before. I may have forgotten my previous recognition that Bobby's interpersonal, intrapersonal, and artistic abilities are well above Billy's. But perhaps more seriously, I may have lost the recognition that both Billy and Bobby are complex persons whom I can never know completely, and I may have lost the ambiguity that should characterize my perception of them. And I may be unaware that Bobby was awake with a family crisis all night before he took the IQ test.

Our third benefit of measurement was that it provides a mechanism for identifying error. An adequate theory of error recognition has proven difficult for scientists and philosophers of science to develop. If two people take a meter stick and make the same measurement, they are very unlikely to obtain the same result. They immediately attribute the result to measurement error, rather than claim that the length is actually different for the two of them. But such an agreement is often lacking in areas that social scientists want to study. What makes agreement on methods for measuring length possible? The best answer available now seems to be that, intuitively, the two meter stick users share an underlying theory of length, guaranteeing that the mapping of objects into numbers called lengths is unique, given a particular unit (here, the meter). That is, they firmly believe that length is a property of the object such that differences in measurement have to result from the measurement process not from the object nor the measuring instrument. But measurements performed in the absence of such a theory and by techniques that have no substantive theoretical base are incapable of generating such a belief. Hence, differences in measurement may lead not to doubt about the accuracy of the particular act of measurement but to doubt about the measuring instrument or even to doubt about the uniqueness of the quantity being measured. If enough people develop enough doubt, this can lead to widespread rejection of the measurement technique, to the loss of whatever benefits it might have obtained, and even to a reduction of credibility for the entire scientific enterprise.

Our fourth benefit of measurement was that it enables social justice, at least in the sense of equity. But mismeasures can cause serious inequities. Such inequities are particularly troubling because of the enormous social benefit that can be derived from accurate measures. Consider, for example, the "streaming" of children after elementary school done in Japan, France, China, and other countries. An accurate identification of a child's gifts can be enormously beneficial to the child and the culture by providing him or her an education suitable to those gifts. But misidentification can have lifelong negative consequences. Another critical justice issue associated with measurement is that measurements of people are internalized by those measured and by others who know the result. Inaccurate or misleading measures may result in serious misconceptions. We will return to this point later in this chapter.

Another benefit of effective measurement was that it raises people's confidence in the truthfulness of information being communicated. If measurement of a human quality is poorly done and leads to inconsistencies or doubt, the credibility of science in general, but more likely the social sciences in particular, can be undermined. This harms the general advance of scholarship and its dissemination by reducing people's confidence in its truthfulness.

Our last benefit was that measurement enables finer distinctions than those possible with natural language. Such distinctions are meaningful and often very helpful when the quantity can be measured on a ratio scale as with temperature, length, or time. But when a ratio scale is not appropriate, making such distinctions can be misleading. A familiar example of this is student grade point averages. That is, student grades are awarded on an ordinal scale and represent an approximate measure of a student's knowledge. These ordinal numbers are then treated as if they were cardinal numbers and averaged. But there is no significant difference between GPAs of 3.44 and 3.45, for instance.

In summary, then, there are significant potential social harms in mismeasurement.[1] We wonder how much of the current respect for the scientific study of the physical world, but suspicion of the scientific study of social phenomena, arises from the experience of some of these harmful effects. In the next two sections, we will examine the four requirements for measurement to see how these harmful effects can arise.

Limitations Associated With Definitions

Human phenomena are complex. Consider such important concepts as religiosity, prejudice, social class, poverty, and good will. Some (like good will) have proven so complex that decision makers who speak of them find it difficult to even attempt a definition. Yet precise definition is an essential prerequisite to measurement. One is tempted to reject measurement of such concepts altogether, but the potential benefits of effective measurement are so great that social scientists have not given up. Before we can assess the way that the social sciences have typically addressed this problem, we need to clarify the notion of definition itself.[2]

First, we can distinguish between univocal, equivocal, and analogous uses of words. *Univocal* uses of words are ones for which there is a one-to-one correspondence between the word and its meaning. Few words in ordinary language are used univocally, but scientific and mathematical words are typically used univocally and when they are not, their (unique) meaning ought to be clear from their context. Words are used *equivocally* when they have multiple meanings that may be quite unrelated. For instance, consider the word "can" as used in the sentences "I can do it" and "The beans were preserved in a tin can." *Analogous* uses of a word occur when the same word refers to similar but distinct meanings. For instance, the uses of the word "religious" in "He is a religious man" and "That is a religious hymn" are analogous. The problem social scientists face in producing fruitful definitions is that many ideas they want to address are associated with words that are part of natural language and may have equivocal and analogous uses. But to be used scientifically, such words must be given univocal meanings. Social scientists have two choices: create new words or create special, univocal meanings for old ones. Both approaches are widely used although both are problematic. The introduction of new scientific words restricts understanding of the scientific work to those who have been initiated into its vocabulary. The redefining (or "precising") of old words may lead to misunderstanding and confusion as people retain many of the older connotations of a word in the new, scientific, setting.

Besides these three different uses of words, we need to distinguish three different types of definitions. Once we have these concepts in mind, we will be able to see how the concept of definition is typically used in the social sciences and thus lay a foundation for a critique of measurement in these sciences.

- A *lexical definition* is a dictionary definition—a list of all popular usages of a word.
- An *essential definition* is a definition that has somehow fully captured the "essence" of an idea. Mathematicians, for example, spent many years in the 19th century debating the proper definition of the word "function" before a definition was finally agreed on.

■ An *operational definition* specifies a repeatable procedure by which one can determine whether a given object or event is an instance of a concept being defined.[3]

Mathematical and scientific definitions are typically operational. Mathematical definitions of abstractions aim to be essential and operational. Nevertheless, for social phenomena, definitions that are essential and operational are rare except in disciplines like mathematical economics and management science. The absence of definitions that are operational and essential helps to explain why there is a division in the social sciences between two different approaches: Some scholars choose operational definitions when definitions that are both operational and essential are not available. This enables them to measure and carry out statistical analyses. Other scholars regard such an approach as oversimplifying and misrepresenting. They seek essential definitions even when such definitions cannot be operationalized. Unless definitions that are simultaneously operational and essential can be found, this difference in approaches is inevitable. In fact, both approaches are necessary.

Scientific and mathematical definitions are closely related to models, as discussed in Chapter 2. That is, when used to describe some real-world phenomenon, they involve simplification and idealization and then formalization of a notion that (one hopes) captures some essential features of a characteristic of interest. Thus, they have the same limitations as models: the price one pays for simplicity, clarity, precision, and tractability is that the concept being defined is removed from context and, by being simplified, is at least partially misrepresented. In a sense then, it is impossible for scientific language to ever represent the truth about social phenomena. In fact, it seems to us that natural language shares the same limitation.

Our focus for the rest of this section will be on operational definitions inasmuch as their formulation typically precedes the production of human information. Operational definitions of real-world entities are positivistic, that is, they are expressed in terms of what can be concretely observed. "Theoretical terms"—terms for things that cannot be directly observed— are allowed, but they must be definable in terms of other things that are directly observable.

Operational definitions are common and familiar. In Chapter 5 we discussed the use of blood alcohol level as a proxy for drunkenness. Defining "drunkenness" as "having a blood alcohol level above .10%, as measured by a breathalyzer" is an operational definition with which most people would feel intuitively comfortable, although they might argue about the choice of .10% as the critical value. Defining social class by various levels of annual income also would be an operational definition but one that would produce considerably less comfort. Defining a city's quality of life is a subtle enterprise, so for the sake of ranking cities, it is operationally defined. Typically such a definition involves a combination of such factors as health, crime, the economy, housing costs, education, transportation, weather, leisure, and the arts. Each of these is operationally defined in a way that yields a numerical measure. These measures are combined into a summary measure that forms the operational definition of "quality of life." Another example of operational definition is ranking of colleges. The magazine *US News and World Report* publishes an annual listing of "best" colleges and universities in various categories. It defines quality as a combination of academic reputation, student selectivity, faculty resources, financial resources, graduation rate, and alumni satisfaction. Each of these factors is measured numerically, some as a composite of several subfactors.

We can gain insight into some difficulties that have arisen in the use of operational definition by examining the history of the notion. The concept of operational definition was introduced in 1927 by P.W. Bridgman, a Harvard University experimental physicist, to address problems in the foundations of physics introduced by Einstein's theory of relativity and by the discovery of quantum mechanics.[4] Discussing length, Bridgman says,

> To find the length of an object, we have to perform certain physical operations. The concept of length is therefore fixed when the operations by which length is measured are fixed: that is, the concept of length involves as much as and nothing more than the set of operations by which length is determined. In general, we mean by any concept nothing more than a set of operations; *the concept is synonymous with the corresponding set of operations.* (p. 5, italics in original)

Thus, applying Bridgman's approach, length is that property of an object that is *defined* by the *act of measuring* it (whether by a meter stick, calipers, or other means).

Bridgman's concept of operational definition has a major weakness, however: It offers no explanation for why there should exist any meaningful correspondence between lengths (so measured) and the real number system. The credibility of the measurement of length as a real number arises from the fact that there is a natural correspondence between the properties of length and the real numbers, that is, lengths combine in the same way that real numbers do and people intuitively recognize this correspondence without needing a formal theory to demonstrate it. In other words, the theory exists whether we formalize it or not and it is the consistency between the theory and the measurement that makes length a socially acceptable and hence useful measurement. It is not sufficient to define length (or any other characteristic) simply by the measurement technique without showing how the technique relates to properties of the characteristic.

We can now see why the use of operational definition has at times caused significant mischief in the social sciences. For instance, terms, such as "intelligence" and "customer satisfaction," can be operationally defined as scores on a test. These terms already have considerable meaning in ordinary language, so people who are not familiar with the technical aspects of the operational definitions assume that their lexical meanings have been made more precise by the operational definition. In fact, this may not be the case. Bridgman himself recognized this difficulty and objected to the use of the term "operational definition" because it claimed too much. Because of this confusion we, along with some other scientists, prefer to replace the term "operational definition" with the more modest term "indicator," as in "quality of life indicator," whenever possible.

A fundamental and extremely important methodological problem underlies this difficulty. Social phenomena are complex and often poorly understood. They are embedded in complex contexts. Thus, understanding requires simplification and idealization and therefore all precise definitions of social phenomena require the use of proxies. Furthermore, to obtain replicable results, operational definitions must be used. Thus, a circularity arises—scientifically defining a concept requires a measurable proxy (so measurement must precede definition), but measurement requires that the concept first be unambiguously defined (so definition must precede measurement).

There is no easy resolution to this dilemma; scientists necessarily work in an artificial world that never quite matches the reality they are trying to study. Their work involves a continual tension.

- On the one hand, the entity one is trying to define is complex and embedded in a complex context. Also, any scientific theory demands unambiguous definition and intersubjective agreement. So operationally defined proxies are necessary.

- On the other hand, operational definitions can be constructed and proxies selected regardless of whether the resulting measurements correspond to the essential character of the entity being measured. Once proxies are selected and an entity is defined operationally, formal analysis can proceed and may continue to some length. But the results obtained may have little or nothing to do with the original concept one was trying to define.

Given this fundamental difficulty, about all social scientists who need to use measurement can do is to develop indicators that capture the essential qualities of a concept as best they can, listen carefully to critics who call attention to the limitations of these indicators, and strive continually to improve the indicators and to understand the essential qualities of the concept. And we all need to continually remind ourselves that we are not actually measuring characteristics like intelligence, customer satisfaction, and quality of life but only proxies for them. That is, in social science our measurements, no matter how precise they may seem, are only as good as our selection of a proxy.

Limitations Associated With Theories, Rankings, and Methods of Measurement

We now look at the three remaining requirements for measurement and see what limitations they place on measurement of human information.

The "theory" requirement is that we have an understanding of the properties of the characteristic of interest that justifies correspondence with our measurement scale. As we saw in the last section, social entities are so complex that normally they are measured via proxies. Thus, the principal danger in the area of theory is that our proxy may satisfy the requirements for measurement whereas the characteristic we actually want to study does not. In this sense the proxy lulls us to sleep and we can begin to confuse the proxy with the actual characteristic.

For example, consider poverty, a complex phenomenon involving many social, cultural, and individual factors. These are difficult to measure so we use a proxy, perhaps gross income. Poverty then is defined as being below a specified income level called a "poverty threshold" or "poverty line." This proxy is indeed a helpful indicator. But if the indicator of poverty is confused with poverty itself, we can be fooled into believing that an intervention to raise income is sufficient to lift someone out of poverty. Note that such an intervention may be helpful—the point is that it is not sufficient because poverty involves social and cultural factors as well as income. Similar considerations apply to two widely used economic indicators: gross national product (GNP) and gross domestic product (GDP). Both are used as proxies for economic well-being, a subtle and poorly defined concept. For example, GNP operationalizes economic well-being as the market value of final sales of products. Thus, GNP is precise and unambiguous. Popular discussions typically refer only to GNP or GDP, not to economic well-being. That is, the proxies have largely replaced the entity—economic well-being—for which they are proxies. But some aspects of economies are not included in GNP or GDP, such as black market activity. Thus, we occasionally hear highly misleading reports, such as the news that the GNP of the former Soviet Union declined 50% per year for three successive years (1991 to 1993) and that it fell 25% in the first quarter of 1994 alone. In fact, much economic activity simply was not reported.

Next we consider limitations in the area of intersubjective ranking. In measuring weight, there is little difficulty with obtaining intersubjective agreement on ranking. If two people each lift two different weights, they will have little difficulty agreeing which is heavier unless the weights are very close. But the social sciences consider human qualities like intelligence, knowledge, customer satisfaction, quality of life, social class, and religiosity. These qualities are so complex that there is little likelihood of intersubjective agreement about which subjects have more of them. As with theory, this difficulty is usually addressed via the use of proxies. For instance, religiosity may be measured by frequency of attendance at a meeting place, such as a church, synagogue, or mosque. But note the same kind of problem we saw with theory: Agreement on a ranking of the proxy may give the illusion of agreement on a ranking of religiosity itself. But such agreement may be short-lived. For example, some classical work on the nature of prejudice found a strong positive correlation between religiosity as measured above and prejudice.[5] Yet subsequent study showed that when intrinsic and extrinsic motives for attending were distinguished, the high correlation only persisted with the extrinsically motivated attenders and not the intrinsically motivated attenders, though the average frequency of attendance was greater for the intrinsically motivated attenders. Thus, the proxy proved inadequate: whereas intersubjective agreement on a ranking of the proxy was easily obtainable (it was measured as a real number), a different proxy gave a different ranking. And a consensus was not immediately forthcoming regarding which best represented religiosity.

The need for a replicable means to measure also places limitations. Here are a few.

■ Sometimes, even when definitions are clear and proxies available, measurement cannot be made. For instance, measurement may be too dangerous, subjects simply may refuse to be interviewed or may insist that the interviewer be an advocate for their concerns before confiding in the interviewer, or collection of data may be more expensive than the researcher can afford.

■ Measurement techniques themselves may have limitations that simply must be acknowledged. Some measurements like blood alcohol level require the use of equipment that can be inaccurate. Some measurements require sampling and so only can be expressed by confidence intervals or by estimates. For example, consider cost of living indices that typically estimate cost of living by pricing items in an artificial "market basket," or student knowledge that is measured by test questions that sample a student's knowledge.

■ Data may be self-reported and therefore inaccurate—subjects may lie or be self-deceived. A classic study of this phenomenon was published by Richard T. LaPiere in 1934.[6] In this study LaPiere described his experiences traveling from 1930 to 1933 with a young Chinese couple. During their travels LaPiere and his Chinese associates approached 67 hotels, auto camps, and tourist homes for accommodation and ate in 184 restaurants or cafes. As much as possible, LaPiere allowed his Chinese guests to enter separately from him. LaPiere recorded detailed observations of the responses of clerks, waiters, and others to himself and his companions. They were only denied service once because of the ethnicity of his companions and they met 11 incidents of hesitancy or something they found temporarily embarrassing. On the other hand, on 97 occasions, LaPiere was treated better than he expected to be treated had he been alone. In the remaining 142 cases, they were treated as expected or treated well but with curiosity. In the second part of his study LaPiere mailed questionnaires to all of the establishments they had visited and asked "Will you accept members of the Chinese race as guests in your establishment?" He obtained a response rate of 51%. Over 90% of the respondents said they would not serve Chinese individuals! LaPiere's conclusion in the same paper was that "it is impossible to make direct comparisons between the reactions secured through questionnaires and from actual experience." He concluded his article with this warning

> The questionnaire is cheap, easy, and mechanical. The study of human behavior is time-consuming, intellectually fatiguing, and depends for its success on the ability of the investigator. The former method gives quantitative results, the latter mainly qualitative. . . . Yet it would seem far more worthwhile to make a shrewd guess regarding that which is essential than to measure that which is likely to prove quite irrelevant. (p. 237)

The normative principle that arises from LaPiere's work is obvious: Questions that ask people what they "would do if" should be avoided.

■ With questions involving categorical or ordinal data, the usefulness of the data depends on the clarity of the categories. For instance, a physical therapist once asked one of the authors of this book to rate the pain he was experiencing on a scale from 0 to 10. He mentally compared his pain to that likely when being crushed to death in an automobile accident and rated his pain a "3." As he found out later, the physical therapist interpreted a 3 as meaning very minor pain and responded by pursuing an inappropriate mode of treatment. This problem (and others like it) easily could be avoided by giving a patient a written list of 10 carefully described scenarios of increasing pain and asking which comes closest to fitting his or her situation. In this way, a shared meaning for the measure would be more likely.

Limitations of Ordinal Scales

One common misuse of measurement that does not arise directly from the four requirements, but should be mentioned, is the inappropriate use of arithmetic operations. As ordinal scales become more common (for good reason—there are many characteristics in the social sciences that do not lend themselves to interval, ratio, or absolute measure), it is frequently forgotten that arithmetic is not meaningful on these scales. For instance, many colleges and universities use a system of faculty evaluation in which students rank a faculty member on an ordinal scale. Typically the student is given a statement, such as "This faculty member presented material in a clear, well-organized fashion." The student then is given response choices on a Likert scale: "1 = strongly agree, 2 = agree, 3 = neutral, 4 = disagree,

5 = strongly disagree." The data are reported to the faculty member with the complete distribution of student responses and a mean score. Oftentimes the mean score is compared to other faculty members' mean scores or an overall institutional mean when making promotion or tenure decisions. But a mean is not an appropriate statistic to calculate for the Likert scale or, in fact, for any ordinal data. Mathematically, the use of a mean requires a scale that is unique up to positive linear transformation, that is, at least an interval scale. More concretely, this means that there is no meaningful sense in which two scores of 2 (for instance) can be equated to one score of 1 plus one score of 3. The appropriate statistic to use for this data is a frequency count. If a one-number summary of the data is desired, the frequency of respondents rating the faculty member at 1 or 2 can be found easily. Because these are absolute data, arithmetic is meaningful and percentages can be calculated. These percentages then can be used meaningfully in decision making. Alternatively, a more comprehensive summary could be given by the cumulative percentages up to each value. Thus a report as (61.2, 90.0, 95.7, 99.0) indicates that 61.2% of the students strongly agreed with the statement, 90.0% at least agreed, 95.7% were not negative, and only 1% strongly disagreed. Only four numbers are needed because the last value will always be 100%.

This critique also applies to student grades, which are typically awarded on such a scale as "A, B, C, D, and F." Such grades are ordinal, not numerical data. Yet typically they are assigned numerical values of 4, 3, 2, 1, and 0 and "grade point averages" (GPA) calculated. This custom probably has persisted because it provides a convenient way to compare students and because it does provide a somewhat meaningful summary of the data—a grade point average near 4.0 means almost all As, whereas a GPA near 2.0 means few As and probably many Cs. But our previous critique still holds—a student with half As and half Cs gets the same GPA as a student with all Bs. But the students' performances are quite different. Still the use of the GPA as a measure of student achievement is probably not too harmful if the entire grade report is examined as well as the GPA and if no major decisions are made on the basis of fine distinctions.

Limitations Arising From Contextual Norms

So far we have focused on methodological norms—those arising from limitations of measurement itself. In this section we ask what limitations are placed on us by contextual norms.

The most obvious limitation of measurement in the social sciences is that controlled experiments with human situations are often nearly impossible or are unethical. When controls cannot be constructed, social science research is not as persuasive as natural science research and causality is difficult to establish, as we shall see in Chapter 8.

But the proscription of controlled experiments on human beings is not the only ethical constraint on measurement of human beings. We mentioned another briefly at the beginning of this chapter, that measurement changes people inasmuch as people internalize measurements performed on them. This internalization changes the persons measured and their relationships with others. Consider, for example, a literacy worker in an impoverished community. She measures the reading level of a man who has completed a sixth-grade education and is respected because of it. She finds he reads at a second-grade level. Her relationship with this man is immediately and irretrievably altered—perhaps for better or worse, but it is changed. When he learns the score, his self-concept will be altered, possibly in harmful ways. His relationship with his school and former teachers also will be changed. Similarly, a child in school who consistently receives word that she scores at the 99th percentile on standardized tests has much of her self-concept and her relationship with her teachers formed by this information. A child who scores below the 10th percentile also will have his or her self-concept and relationships formed but in a very different way. Even groups' self-concepts and relationships are affected by measurement. For instance, the measurement and labeling of groups as "disadvantaged" has resulted in such groups forming an identity and seeking equal treatment.[7] The ethical consequences of such measurements are great even if the measurements are meaningful and accurate. If they are invalid, the potential for harm is enormous.

The medical profession espouses the contextual norm "Do no harm." That norm is applicable to the measurement of human characteristics as well as to medical treatment. Human measurement only should be made after the potential impact on the persons measured has been carefully considered and adequate preparation made to deal with possible negative consequences. Furthermore, educational programs that teach people how to use measurements need to include training in the ethics of dealing with the changes those measurements produce in people.

Contextual norms can enter in another way. The purpose for which a particular measurement is performed can compromise contextual norms. As we discussed in Chapter 4, objectivity is a limiting ideal that is never fully attainable. But objectivity is sometimes ignored altogether. For instance, evaluation of a project often becomes an unpleasant necessity to keep grant money flowing. In such cases what is measured, how it is measured, and what is reported all are subordinate to a goal other than truthfulness, which is certainly a contextual norm.

Two further limitations arise from the fact that measurement is performed in a social context.

1. Human information, no matter how carefully and accurately gathered, often requires a discussion of values and principles before meaningful interpretation is possible. For instance, consider the unemployment rate. A cartoon portrayed a statistician reporting that his research had shown that a 7% unemployment rate was acceptable to 93% of the people. The 7% rate cannot be given a meaningful interpretation apart from values and principles that determine what unemployment rate is acceptable. Selection of such values and principles requires some societal discussion.

2. The impact of human information is never neutral, as it is reported in a context that involves human preconceptions, values, and beliefs. For instance, if a school official announces that 70% of the children enrolled in Franklin Delano Roosevelt High School are minority students, the 70% figure is reported on an absolute scale and involves no proxies, so it seems neutral. But it is received in a context in which there are multiple assumptions about the nature of Franklin Delano Roosevelt High School, many judgments about what constitutes an appropriate proportion of minority enrollment, and many different understandings of the word "minority." In short, a simple, apparently objective piece of human data has enormously different meanings to different people. Reporters and users of such data need to consider the context in which they will be reported.

CASE STUDIES

We conclude this chapter with three case studies that will suggest how normative thinking in the conduct of social science can be done and be helpful.

Intelligence

Although the measurement of intelligence has a somewhat sordid history, it began with noble objectives. Alfred Binet (1857-1911), whose name has been attached to one of the most famous IQ tests, the Stanford-Binet test, was commissioned in Paris in 1904 to conduct a very practical study: to find means of identifying children who would not be successful in regular classrooms but could benefit from some form of special education. Binet developed a test with a large number of short tasks related to everyday problems of life and graded these in order of difficulty. He included tasks suitable for many different ages. A child's "mental age" then was identified by the number of tasks he or she could complete. After Binet's death, this mental age was converted to an "intelligence quotient" by dividing it by the child's chronological age and multiplying by 100. The test score is thus an operational definition of intelligence.

After Binet's work, IQ testing began in the United States and intelligence was hypothesized to be genetically related. Differences in the scores of ethnic and racial groups surfaced and these were used as arguments for the inherent superiority or inferiority of different groups. In perhaps the worst abuse of measurement known, during the 1930s Jewish refugees who anticipated trouble with the Hitler regime sought to emigrate to the United States but were denied. The grounds were that, on the basis of IQ test scores, they were genetically inferior. Controversies about racial and ethnic links to intelligence have periodically resurfaced, as in the publication of *The Bell Curve* by Richard Herrnstein and Charles Murray in 1994. In this book the authors point out that African Americans score an average of about 15 points below white Americans on IQ tests. The book's most controversial feature is a claim that between 40% and 80% of this difference can be attributed to genetic factors.

In this section we want to examine only the measurement of intelligence; we will return to causative explanations of IQ differences in Chapter 8. We hope to demonstrate that the analytic techniques we have presented can help us understand why the history of intelligence measurement has been so controversial and also help make some normative judgments about the measurement and use of IQ.

Note the situation: Although intelligence has been widely studied since the 19th century (and reflected on much earlier), there does not exist a widely agreed-on theory of intelligence. But there are strong incentives to measure intelligence. Societies would like to enable their most able young people to be well trained, employers would like to be able to select the most able employees from applicants, militaries would like to identify potential officers, and colleges would like to select the most promising applicants. Thus, a test that is easily administered and yields a numerical score is very attractive. So again, we encounter the temptation to cut corners.

There have been three main approaches to the study of intelligence. The approach that has been the basis of IQ testing after Binet sees intelligence primarily as a single mental factor, usually denoted g, for "general intelligence." The evidence for g began with the work of Charles Spearman in 1904. Spearman developed a statistical technique, called factor analysis, to aid in distinguishing the number of distinct "factors" in a collection of multiattribute data. That is, suppose an intelligence test consists of a collection of a dozen subtests (for instance, vocabulary, geometric visualization, etc.), each subtest consisting of closely related questions. A student is awarded a score on each of the 12 subtests and each subtest is then regarded as one attribute. Students who score well on one subtest tend to do well on other subtests also, so scores on the subtests tend to be correlated. Factor analysis enables the identification of one or more principal components that make up these scores. Note that the components identified are mathematical abstractions; they may or may not correspond to anything real. Nevertheless, because IQ test scores consistently yield a single dominant component, that component has been reified and called g.

Recent work by Howard Gardner represents a second approach to understanding the nature of intelligence. Gardner argued for seven distinct intelligences: linguistic, musical, logical-mathematical, spatial, bodily-kinesthetic, interpersonal, and intrapersonal. Other scholars have argued for an even larger number of distinct intelligences.

A third approach is that of Jean Piaget. Piaget started his career in Binet's laboratory in Paris around 1919, after Binet had died. He quickly turned his studies away from the quantitative measure of intelligence to the study of the underlying structure of intelligence. In Piaget's view, which he called genetic epistemology, human intellect develops through a sequence of four main stages, with many substages. These stages have the same basic form, independent of culture. The different stages represent different types of reasoning.

We are now at the point at which we can conduct a normative analysis of IQ: *The principal methodological problem is that IQ tests measure intelligence on a numerical scale, but at present there exists no theoretical justification for a correspondence between intelligence and numbers.* That is, IQ scores for an individual are typically relatively consistent over time and are often correlated (or inversely correlated) with other important factors, such as income, social class, and rates of out-of-wedlock births. Thus, they are indeed measuring something important. But because IQ scores are not based on a meaningful concept of intelligence and because no one has demonstrated that intelligence corresponds to numerical values, IQ tests cannot properly be called "intelligence tests." Herrnstein and Murray[8] partially recognized this critique and dismissed it.

> Before something can be measured, it must be defined, this argument goes. And the problems of definition for beauty, justice, or intelligence are insuperable. To people who hold these views, the claims of the intelligence testers seem naive at best or vicious at worst. These views . . . are generally advanced primarily by non-specialists. (pp. 17-18)

After this comment Herrnstein and Murray did not return to the critique and wrote another 645 pages. But the critique cannot be diminished this lightly, especially when one considers the enormous social harm that IQ measurements have been used to justify. Even Binet was acutely conscious of the limitation we have addressed here. Writing about his intelligence scale in 1905, Binet[9] asserted, "The scale, properly speaking, does not permit the measure of the intelligence, because intellectual qualities are not superposable, and therefore cannot be measured as linear surfaces are measured."

The application of factor analysis to the study of IQ test scores is also problematic. Factor analysis of intelligence test scores simply identifies the existence of a dominant factor; it does not tell us what that factor is. Spearman and others have interpreted this result as unitary intelligence, g. But, as we saw in Chapter 4, such an interpretation is heavily dependent on the presuppositions one brings to the act of interpreting. For instance, the dominant factor just as well could be interpreted as symbol manipulation skill, because all of the tests depend on the test taker's capacity to manipulate verbal, visual, or oral symbols. That is, the case for g is far from conclusive.

Contextual norms also help to analyze the measurement of intelligence. Some commonsensical norms that clearly apply are respect for persons, service to others, compassion, and stewardship of human resources. From the point of view of these principles, intelligence testing was originally well-intentioned, but its subsequent use at times has been deplorable. It has been used to select an elite group and to justify discriminatory practices toward those who are judged inferior (as in the 1930s). Such uses obviously violate all of these norms.

In conclusion, it is clear that IQ tests are measuring something. It is not so clear what that something is. Calling it "intelligence" is dishonest, inasmuch as no theoretical foundation has been advanced to demonstrate a correspondence between any definition of intelligence (other than the operational definition: "Intelligence is what IQ tests are measuring.") and an IQ score. Nevertheless, we do not want to exclude all mental measurements. For instance, SAT and ACT (American College Testing service) tests have proven to be moderately effective indicators of potential success in college. Thus, they provide a means for colleges to compare students from different high schools. When used for this purpose and in conjunction with other indicators, such as high school grades, recommendations, and personal interviews, they can be genuinely helpful. Such measures as IQ scores also can be helpful in decisions, such as finding appropriate educational programs for slow learners, if we recognize the limitations of IQ scores and use them in conjunction with other data and personal knowledge of the test taker.

Stress

One influential study in psychology is the work of Thomas Holmes and Richard Rahe on stress.[10] Holmes and Rahe were studying the link between stress and illness. From their clinical experience, they compiled a list of 43 life events that they judged to be stressful, that is, that required individuals to make significant psychological adjustments to adapt to the event. Then they asked 394 subjects to rate the stressfulness of these events on a numerical scale. The following instructions were given to each subject.[11]

In scoring, use all of your experience in arriving at an answer. This means personal experience where it applies as well as what you have learned to be the case for others. Some persons accommodate more readily to change than others; some persons adjust with particular ease or difficulty to only certain events. Therefore, strive to give your opinion of the average degree of adjustment necessary for each event rather than the extreme. . . . "Marriage" has been given an arbitrary value of 500. As you complete each of the remaining events, think to yourself, "Is this event indicative of more or less readjustment than marriage? Would the readjustment take longer or shorter to accomplish?" (p. 173)

TABLE 6.1 The Social Readjustment Rating Scale

Rank	Life Event	Mean Value
1	Death of spouse	100
2	Divorce	73
3	Marital separation	65
4	Jail term	63
5	Death of close family member	63
6	Personal injury or illness	53
7	Marriage	50
8	Fired at work	47
9	Marital reconciliation	45
10	Retirement	45
11	Change in health of a family member	44
12	Pregnancy	40
13	Sex difficulties	39
14	Gain of new family member	39
15	Business readjustment	39
16	Change in financial state	38
17	Death of a close friend	37
18	Change to different line of work	36
19	Change in number of arguments with spouse	35
20	Mortgage over $10,000	31
21	Foreclosure on mortgage or loan	30
22	Change in responsibilities at work	29

The ratings of the 43 events then were averaged, the mean was divided by 10, and rounded to the nearest whole number. The results are given in Table 6.1.

Note that the dollar amounts in items 20 and 37 reflect 1967 prices. To use the Social Readjustment Rating Scale (SRRS), an individual circles the items on the list that have occurred in his or her life in the previous 12 months and totals the points assigned to those items, giving a score in "life change units" (LCUs); this score then is regarded as a measure of the amount of stress a person has experienced in the previous 12 months.

Subsequent to the development of the SRRS, statistical analysis showed that correlating a person's LCU score with health indicators only accounts for about 10% of the variation in health. Furthermore, the scale has been critiqued on several grounds: It includes positive and negative events in the

TABLE 6.1 *Continued*

Rank	Life Event	Mean Value
23	Son or daughter leaving home	29
24	Trouble with in-laws	29
25	Outstanding personal achievement	28
26	Wife begin or stop work	26
27	Begin or end school	26
28	Change in living conditions	25
29	Revision of personal habits	24
30	Trouble with boss	23
31	Change in work hours or conditions	20
32	Change in residence	20
33	Change in schools	20
34	Change in recreation	19
35	Change in church activities	19
36	Change in social activities	18
37	Mortgage or loan less than $10,000	17
38	Change in sleeping habits	16
39	Change in number of family get-togethers	15
40	Change in eating habits	15
41	Vacation	13
42	Christmas	12
43	Minor violations of the law	11

same scale. It includes events over which a person has control along with events over which a person has no control, although research has shown that sudden, negative, uncontrollable events are far more effective predictors of illness than positive, controllable events. It does not take into account the meaning of the event to the person. For example, a planned pregnancy has a very different stress effect than an unplanned one. Many of the items also are vague. But despite these criticisms, the SRRS has stimulated much research and has been given a great deal of attention in popular magazines and newspapers.

The techniques for normative analysis of measurement we have presented here can, we believe, enable an additional useful critique of the SRRS. First, note how the scale was established. The SRRS is a ratio scale in that two fixed points—marriage as a 500 and absence of stress as a 0—were established, and values were assigned to other events in relation to the two fixed points. (Although the 0 was not explicitly mentioned in the directions to subjects, it is implicit in the comparison to 500. That is, subjects are judging what fraction of 500 corresponds to a particular stressor, thus rating on a scale with fixed points of 0 and 500.) Once a ratio scale has been established many capabilities follow, though the only one used by Holmes and Rahe is additivity. For instance, if the ratio scale is valid, one can meaningfully say that foreclosure of a mortgage or loan is twice as stressful as change in number of family get-togethers. Also, the incremental stress of death of a spouse as compared to divorce is the same as the incremental stress of an outstanding personal achievement over a minor violation of the law. We suspect that most persons would be uncomfortable with these multiplicative and incremental comparisons and, in fact, Holmes and Rahe don't make them. But these operations are intrinsic in use of a ratio scale; if we are skeptical about these operations, we ought also be skeptical about the additivity that Holmes and Rahe did use.

Let's examine the SRRS in the light of the four requirements for measurement. First, as critics have pointed out, there are serious definitional problems. Holmes and Rahe defined stress as the need for psychological readjustment to an event. This is not an operational definition but rather an attempt at an essential definition. But common lexical definitions include stressful states (not just change) and distinguish stress caused by negative events from stress caused by positive events. Furthermore many of the events listed are described ambiguously. So the likelihood of a socially useful measure of stress is diminished by the somewhat nonstandard definition of stress that Holmes and Rahe used and by the inconsistent interpretations of the events likely to result from their ambiguous descriptions. Even so, this in itself does not make the measure socially useless or harmful—recall how social class still maintains some usefulness as a concept despite its ambiguous definition.

The second requirement for measurement is intersubjective agreement on ranking. Unfortunately, this important requirement was finessed by simply averaging the subjects' scores. Considerably more insight into stress could have been gained by examining subjects' rankings of the stress-producing events, doing correlational studies of the lists of rankings, identifying when there was strong agreement and disagreement, and discussing areas of disagreement with subjects to find out why they perceived the stressors differently.

The third requirement is a theory of the properties of the entity being studied that justifies its correspondence with the desired scale. From our perspective, this is the major weakness of the SRRS. The authors began by assuming the appropriateness of a ratio scale and then asked subjects to rate stressors relative to fixed points. But the essential prior question of the appropriateness of this scale was not addressed. Why should one assume that stress is one-dimensional? Stress may have multiple components that affect health in different ways. It is not difficult to conceive of the notion that certain types of stressors cause ulcers, others cause headaches, and others affect the immune system. Such a notion may or may not be correct, but an analysis of the structure of stress must precede the establishment of a numerical measure. Furthermore, Holmes and Rahe assume additivity when they use a ratio scale. But we see no *a priori* reasons to believe that stresses are linearly additive. Stresses may combine in a multiplicative fashion; perhaps some people are able to discount the effect of additional stressors in some fashion. Whatever the case may be, the assumption of a simple linear additive model is unwarranted.

And last, the measuring instrument is vulnerable to the critique that "What would you do if " type questions are being asked. We have seen in the discussion of Richard LaPiere's work that such questions are notoriously unreliable.

The SRRS is a good example of "corner cutting"—trying to gain the benefits of a numerical measure without paying the price of the substantive theoretical work required to determine whether such a measure is appropriate. But what about contextual norms? Can they add anything further to our understanding of the SRRS? Our main concern is the potential harm to the credibility of measurement in the social sciences resulting from the use of a poorly grounded measuring instrument like the SRRS; many people intuitively recognize it as an oversimplification, even without understanding the foundations of measurement.

Project Evaluation

In this case study we examine an evaluation technique commonly used by granting agencies. Our example here is based on an actual agency, but the details have been modified to preserve anonymity. We call our (fictitious) agency Third World Economic Development (TWED).

TWED's long range strategic plan states: "Our vision is to enable and empower people to undertake independent responses such that the poor and their community flourish." It also identifies its "core values" as stewardship of natural resources, independence, and justice. These terms are not explicitly defined and this causes some problems, as we shall see.

TWED is quite explicit about its goals, objectives, and the strategies it uses to achieve them. Its international objective is "To serve 100,000 families in poverty bringing them toward self-sufficiency, to help organize local community groups, and to work with established organizations enabling them to independently identify and resolve their own community problems and needs." TWED employs five strategies to achieve these goals.

1. Organizational development and collaborative planning (providing consult-ation for other similar agencies)
2. Community development (training and leadership development, increasing income through food production or small industry, improving health care largely through preventive measures, and increasing functional literacy rates)
3. Leadership development (training local groups to provide assistance)
4. Disaster response (direct aid, refugee resettlement)
5. Constituency participation (volunteer programs, on-site visits)

TWED uses a somewhat informal approach to select new sites at which to apply the previous five strategies. Nevertheless, once a site has been selected TWED uses quantitative methods in its ongoing planning for that site. A single "international planning form" is used with minor variations at several levels of planning—the individual local site, the country, and the project (a collection of local sites within a country). It consists of four parts and is completed annually by staff directly involved at each level. The first part is a simple summary of dates (when the project was begun and when it is expected to become independent), other organizations involved, and anticipated cost. The second part asks the evaluator to assess either the community in which the project is being conducted or the organization conducting the project. Table 6.2 is a copy of this second part for a community. It is explained below.

The third part of the international planning form asks about the number of families involved and requests some financial data, including cost per family. Part four asks for specific objectives for the project. These differ, depending on the nature of the project. For example, on health care it asks for the number of children from ages 0 to 6 and the number of families to which they belong, the current death and malnutrition rates, and the target rates at the site.

TABLE 6.2 TWED Community Capacity Indicators

Organizational Capacity Indicators	92	93	94	95	96	97	Levels of Independence
Technical							5 = independent
Management (incl. financial)							4 = adequate quality
Networking and Resource Development							3 = needs improvement/ cooperation
Board Control							2 = unsatisfactory results
Holistic Outreach							1 = not functioning
Average							

Once these data have been collected, they are used to make a variety of comparisons, such as site to site within the country, country to country, and project director to project director. Comparisons are not made mechanically by, for instance, comparing average scores. Effort is made to look at the entire assessment and to take different contexts into account.

We now have enough information to evaluate this measurement technique. We will focus primarily on the community capacity table. Note that the measurement scale being used for each indicator is an ordinal scale. As pointed out earlier in this chapter, there are two requirements for using an ordinal scale: unambiguous definitions (both of the indicator being measured and of the scale categories) and intersubjective agreement on rankings.

First, we consider definitional issues. Table 6.2 serves as an operational definition of quality for TWED—the five indicators constitute five equally weighted aspects of quality. Nevertheless, the five indicators also operationally define the core values on which TWED bases its work, despite the long-range plan's core values of stewardship, independence, and justice. That is, inasmuch as decisions on funding and staff performance evaluation are made primarily on the basis of scores earned on the five indicators, these indicators, not the list of core values, serve as the primary guides for the work of project directors. These two sets of values are not necessarily inconsistent, but the existence of two statements of values, one of which is operationalized and one of which is not, may be confusing and could result in a misapplication of the work. In fact, looking over the five indicators and the measurement scale, one would conclude that TWED's core values actually are operational effectiveness (which could be interpreted as stewardship) and independence. It is not clear how justice is being operationalized.

We don't want to be overly critical of TWED on this point. The observation we have just made—of a potential difference between an organization's explicitly stated values, goals, or both and the operational definitions that actually guide its decision making—is extremely common. Nevertheless, it would be wise for any organization to think carefully about whether a gap exists between the two.

Given the use of these five indicators of quality, we next must ask if they are unambiguously defined. Explicit definitions are not stated for them, but implicit definitions are given in a separate questionnaire in which evaluators are asked a series of questions grouped under the headings of the five indicators. For instance, under "technical capacity" questions are asked about staff expertise and creativity, experience working with target groups, and assessment of community problems, needs, and priorities. Each question asks for a response on a five-point scale where "1 = not functioning, 2 = unsatisfactory, 3 = needs improvement, 4 = adequate, and 5 = excellent." For the indicator "management," 22 such questions are asked; under "networking," two are asked. Under each of "board control" and "holistic outreach," three questions are asked. The vast difference in the number of questions asked in each category suggests that in fact management capacity may be the most important of the five factors to the TWED staff. But the summative instrument does not reflect this and the averaging process treats them equally.

The key definitional issue is whether all TWED evaluators and their supervisors understand the terms in the same way. The questions help a great deal to communicate this common understanding. But it could be enhanced even more by succinct, explicit definitions. Staff training also could help; we will comment more on this point later.

Another definitional problem is that the constituency may not agree with TWED's definition of quality, particularly if the constituency is defined broadly enough to include the poor with whom TWED is working. Without an agreement on the definition of quality, measurement of it is meaningless. That is, North American staff can form an operational definition and can train field personnel to use it. But at least some people in the many diverse cultures the field staff work with are likely to have quite a different concept of quality. This is especially critical because TWED's goal statements place a high value on independence. Hence, there is a potential inconsistency between the relatively well-defined operational definition TWED has formed and its value of independence. One possible resolution of this inconsistency is to allow local cultures to modify the definition in dialogue with TWED staff. A common definition throughout the organization does provide a great benefit by providing for common understanding. But because it originates with the granting agency, it may not serve the goal of independence.

Beyond these problems of definition, use of an ordinal scale such as the one TWED has used requires intersubjective agreement on the meaning of the five levels on which each indicator is ranked. The TWED scale has some problems here. Most serious is the ambiguous definition of the five levels.

Unfortunately, people's intuitions in complex situations as those being evaluated by TWED vary a great deal. Thus, explicit instruction is needed to ensure meaningful intersubjective agreement. This could take several forms.

- Explicit definition of the categories "Excellent," "Adequate Quality," and so forth
- Metaphors, such as "Ripe," "Sprouting," "Newly Seeded," and so forth
- Preparation of a list of scenarios that illustrate each of the five levels for at least some of the five indicators. An evaluator could look at the scenarios and say "Now which of these come closest to fitting my situation?"
- Explicit training for staff in the use of the planning form. Training might best be done with sample case studies that could be evaluated by staff and then discussed.

Even if there were intersubjective agreement on the definitions of the categories, there remains a problem with the use of the average at the bottom of Table 6.2. Granting agencies frequently use ordinal scales similar to the scale used by TWED, then average the scores on different indicators. Such an average has the decided benefit of being an easily computed summary measure. But it is technically meaningless because the data are not quantitative. Consider two sites. Suppose one is rated an "excellent" (5) on one indicator and a "not functioning" (1) on another. The second site is rated "needs improvement" (3) on both. The average for each site is a 3 and hence the method equates these two sites. But there is no meaningful sense in which they are equal. A better summary measure is the frequency count (for example, "This site rated two excellents and three adequates"). Alternatively, a vector listing the frequencies at each level, such as (2,3,0,0,0) could be used. The choice of a summary measure depends on the values of an organization. In some settings, high quality performance in a few areas is very important, whereas poor performance in other areas can be overlooked. In such a situation, a frequency count of the "excellents" would be a good measure. In other situations good performance across all categories is of great importance. In such a case, the frequency of "excellents" plus the frequency of "adequates" might be a good measure; a penalty could even be assessed for low scores by subtracting their frequency.

It also would be wise for TWED to drop the numbers associated with the levels because numbers are normally interpreted as cardinal values rather than ordinal values—stating the levels as numbers immediately introduces the temptation to do arithmetic on them. Even using the letters A, B, C, D, and E should be avoided inasmuch as these letters are so commonly converted to numbers and averaged in schools. It would be better to use verbal descriptors like "exc," "adeq," "nimp," "unsat," and "nf" that have no natural numerical associations yet still allow for frequency counts.

The use of quantitative objectives (as in the fourth part of the form) is helpful, but, as TWED itself has realized, the indicators selected are short-term and do not necessarily measure sustainable changes after the project is completed. They represent "output" rather than "outcome" changes. TWED is currently working to replace these with more long term measures.

In summary, then, a measurement-based approach to evaluation is a helpful tool for assessing quality. Nevertheless, because such a tool operationalizes the values of the organization, considerable care must be exercised in selecting the right proxies for quality. That is, the indicators selected must accurately represent the values of the organization. Such a tool also requires clear definitions shared by all evaluators and requires significant effort to ensure intersubjective agreement on rankings. Finally, in a situation like TWED's in which sites are located in many different cultures and involve many different types of projects, local variations in definitions of quality are needed, even though this causes some difficulties with communication.

■ NOTES

1. For some astounding examples of mismeasures in the area of intelligence that had serious consequences, see Gould (1981).

2. For our discussion of definition in this section, we are very much indebted to Professor John Edelman of the Philosophy Department of Nazareth College of Rochester, NY. His unpublished manuscript explicating these ideas more fully is available on request. The college's address is 4245 East Ave., Rochester, NY, 14624.

3. For those interested in a concrete example of a definition that is simultaneously essential and operational, the word *function* is defined by mathematicians as follows: Let A be a set, B be a set, and consider a set of ordered pairs of the form (a,b) where a is a member of A and b is a member of B. The three sets are a function if every a in A corresponds to one and only one b in B.

4. See Bridgman (1927).

5. See Allport (1958).

6. LaPiere (1934, pp. 230-237).

7. See the article by Guillemin and Horowitz, Section 10.3.c in Callahan and Jennings (1983).

8. Herrnstein and Murray (1994).

9. As quoted in Gould (1981, p. 151).

10. See Holmes and Rahe (1967). For a clear summary and evaluation of Holmes and Rahe's work see Hock (1992).

11. Holmes and Rahe (as quoted in Hock, 1992, p. 213).

Information
for Inferences

What *Are* Social Science Data?

■ INTRODUCTION:
WHAT ARE WE STUDYING?

Janet, Laura, and Fran carpool each day to their jobs in the city.

Janet is an experimental physicist at a major university. Most of her day is spent constructing experimental equipment or sitting at a computer terminal analyzing the data generated by this equipment, though she occasionally relies on the published data of other researchers. Before beginning a study, she carefully identifies the relevant theories that might influence her observations, specifies the type of data that would be necessary to test a hypothesis about these theories, builds equipment that will generate such data while controlling for other things that the theory indicates might also influence the variables being studied, and specifies which types of observations would render her theory false. One full day

137

each week is devoted to keeping current with the professional literature and writing up the results of her work.

Fran is a police detective. She spends much of her work time carefully searching crime scenes for information that seemed insignificant on the first approach, or reviewing forensic lab reports on the data collected at the crime scene. She constantly is trying to reframe her topic from different angles, searching for the explanation of events that seems most plausible and best supported by all the different constructions that might be put on the information available. She always asks herself, "Where am I too self-assured in my theory? How might a different investigator put this together? Where have my value judgments influenced my work, and are these defensible influences? What will the judge and jury think?" Because it is difficult to prove her hypotheses without a confession, she prepares to submit them to peers who will judge their "reasonable doubtfulness." Whereas the scientific lab work is helpful, her peers rarely accept it as conclusive—it is the plausibility of the explanation connected to the lab work that makes it credible or incredible.

Laura is a business consultant with a strong mathematics background. Her daily work ranges over all of the social sciences. It includes estimating demand curves, conducting sociological studies for marketing initiatives, administering psychological testing for human resources departments, characterizing voting behavior for political action clients, consulting with school boards on interpreting data in studies of teaching effectiveness, providing advice on business process engineering, and giving expert legal testimony for lost-earnings lawsuits. She is an applied-social-scientist-of-all-trades. Much of her daily work consists of using computerized statistical packages and spreadsheets to analyze published governmental or social-scientific survey data and then presenting the results in a comprehensible form.

Each of these three friends is involved in classifying, generating, and interpreting data, in the hope of explaining events. Of the three professions, which two have the most in common?

If we glanced through the texts Laura, the social scientist, used in college, we would get the impression that she was trained to be a people physicist. The statistical tools she lives by—regressions, ANOVA tables, tests of hypotheses, confidence intervals, and so forth—were borrowed from the natural sciences. Social science results are presented in a form similar to the physical sciences, in style of writing and in presentation of statistical tests. And there is very little of the detective in the way Laura gathers her data; she analyzes published or survey data in much the same way a physicist analyzes the output of a piece of equipment. She is rarely concerned with the constant reframing of her approach that preoccupies Fran, the detective.

But is this appropriate? Does Laura's "scientific" habit serve the best interests of her clients and profession? The answer largely turns on the answer to another set of questions: Are the data of the social sciences more like the data of physics or the data of a detective investigation? What are the nature and character of social-scientific data? Once we have considered these questions, we will be in a better position to evaluate the ways that statistical tools are used by social scientists—inferential statistics in this chapter and methods that explore causality in the next.

NONEXPERIMENTAL DATA FROM COMPLEX SITUATIONS

We have seen in Chapters 5 and 6 that all three types of analysis—natural science, social science, and detective work—face a set of difficulties in measurement. But there are measurement problems that seem especially typical of social science work. Consider first the fundamental thing that most of the work of the social scientist and the detective have in common. Both work with what we might call "nonexperimental" data.[1] Rarely does either analyst have the luxury of using data generated by a process the investigator designed to assure standardized data controlled for extraneous influences. Social scientists and detectives receive information from a nonstandardizable environment that was not designed nor controlled by them.

Combine this with the fact that the activities generating the information are nonrepeatable and nonreplicable, and we are in a difficult position. Fran cannot say, "Let's run that murder again without the victim's financial problems last month," to narrow her list of hypotheses. Nor can Laura repeat her marketing survey under a different configuration of interest rates and unemployment statistics. Neither professional can create defendable "controls" for the issue she wishes to study.

Even if social scientists had experimental data,[2] because of the general nature of social relationships (i.e., the matter being studied), it is difficult to obtain data that isolate the phenomenon under study from the effects of the general environment. If we want to test the theory that X influences Y, we must convert this idea into a measurable, mathematically testable form. As we have argued, the standards for being "measurable" depend on what kind of measurement scale we hope to use. We need at least a clear, unambiguous definition of the characteristic under study. But we have argued that clarity of definition depends on having a well-developed theory of the characteristic and a good measurement technique for the characteristic or (in cases when the characteristic is not directly measurable) a well-developed theory of the relationship between the things that *can* be measured and the characteristics in our theory.

Yet the very complexity of social relationships, the difficulty of disentangling a cause from the simultaneous circumstantial changes elsewhere in the social fabric of life, makes development of precise measurement techniques and theories difficult. We have argued that for much of the social sciences this implies that either (a) definitions are somewhat "fuzzy," requiring humility in claims about our ability to measure and an admission that we lack complete objectivity in framing our work, or (b) a dose of subtlety in choosing the measurement scale that is appropriate to our characteristic. Social scientists are inclined, out of a desire to make the characteristic under study follow the intuitive properties of the real numbers, to presume use of an interval or ratio scale when a nominal or ordinal scale may press the limits of our definitions.

These two implications are interrelated: The fuzziness of social science definitions also seems to encourage a jump to measurement before the characteristic being considered is really understood.

MODELING AND IRREFUTABILITY

Because of the imprecision of definitions, the inability to directly measure some characteristics (call them X and Y), or the lack of availability of the most-preferred data, analysts often need to choose proxies for X and Y, variables that *can* be measured, whose behavior imitates that of X and Y in a predictable manner. One then must choose a particular data set from among those several that are often available.[3] In experimental and nonexperimental situations, one must identify and model other influential factors (but only the most influential ones, to keep the problem tractable) and hope that they are also measurable on a scale that is precise enough to make the conclusions meaningful. In many cases (such as regression analysis) a specific form of the function relating X and Y then must be chosen for testing.

All these operations are required if we are to isolate the phenomenon under study from the effects of the general environment. But any one of these operations could be done with error, and correcting an error at any of these points could change the conclusion of the study. Thus, when social scientists conduct a study of whether X affects Y, the study must test the measurement and abstractions of the analysis besides testing the relationship between the two characteristics; there must be some perpetual skepticism about the accuracy of the measurement instruments, the quality of the theory of the characteristics under study, and the clarity of definition of the characteristics being studied.

A short illustration may be helpful.

A professor asks her students to study "whether . . . race [is] a significant factor in the processing and outcome of . . . homicide cases [in the United States]," the aim of a classic paper by Radelet.[4] The original paper proceeded by studying the extent to which the death penalty is assigned for particular types of homicides. Our professor supplies students with some of the data reported by Radelet.[5] Though race is a difficult attribute to measure, Radelet coded a number of cases in 20 of Florida's 67 counties in 1976 and 1977 as involving either blacks or whites. Information on sex, age, and criminal record of victims and defendants was not available in the original paper and is not provided to the students.

Student Number One organizes the available information in this way:

	White defendant	*Black defendant*
Death penalty	19	17
No death penalty	141	149

As there is no significant difference between the white and black cells, he concludes that the system must be pretty fair. In fact, a higher proportion of white defendants were sentenced to death.

Student Number Two organizes the available data in this way:

| | White defendant Death penalty | | Black defendant Death penalty | |
	Y	N	Y	N
White victim	19	132	11	52
Black victim	0	9	6	97

Student Number Two comes to a different conclusion: For all victims, a significantly higher percentage of black defendants are sentenced to death. This insight was, in fact, central to the findings in the original paper.[6]

Despite the apparent clarity of the numbers, it is still not certain that we actually know much about the fairness of the criminal justice system. It could in fact be even less fair than either approach indicates. We have a data set that is quite limited geographically, temporally, and "judicially"— only one sentence for one crime is considered—and the crucial variable, race, is a notoriously difficult one to define. The model probably does not account for enough influential factors; whereas race of victim seems a reasonable variable to include (and thus the second student's result seems more reasonable), we have not yet controlled for previous criminal records nor gender differences. Yet including a proxy for "previous criminal record," given the complex variety among such histories, would involve some very rough generalizations that might leave us even less secure about the results. And if the problems in controlling for previous record were solved by finding a reasonable index, inadvertently we would be assuming the result we aim to investigate. We would test the fairness of the judicial system by assuming that all previous convictions were fair. Thus, the model inadvertently would bias our work toward concluding that the system is just.

Let us be clear about our intentions. We do not aim to dispute Radelet's conclusions about whether and how race is significant in the U.S. justice system. Rather, we are illustrating how difficult it is to come to firm conclusions in social science research.

Now, let us say all of this differently. To test any primary hypothesis in a complex social situation with nonexperimental data, we must swallow a large group of auxiliary hypotheses on related issues (such as being able to ignore previous criminal record). If our study yields a falsification of our original theory (in this case, that the system is fair), we will have a difficult time disentangling a failure of the main hypothesis from a failure of one of the peripheral hypotheses. Thus, we will have difficulty coming to a firm conclusion. The variation in Y from what was anticipated could indicate that our theory about X is untrue, but it also could indicate measurement problems of the observations or the initial conditions, or poor controls, misspecification of the model (deleted variables or improper abstraction and modeling), errors in choosing proxies, or (when the analysis involves estimating coefficients in equations) misspecifications of the functional form. Whereas we might hope that knowledge generally proceeds by finding falsifications of earlier presumptions, the complexity of social realities implies that we will rarely get a clear falsification of any claim. Like a bad sheriff who can always slant the evidence to implicate the person he is out to get, there will always be a ready excuse (in the form of a failed auxiliary hypothesis) if an analyst's favorite theory appears to be falsified by the data.

This is known as Duhem's irrefutability thesis. With respect to many social science theories, there are no definitive counterfacts. There are no conclusive tests, and we can never be sure our tentatively corroborated theories are the best possible. Main hypotheses are insulated from hard rejections.

To say this in more general terms, observations usually require interpretation before being useful. Whether we even count a variable or event as an observation is affected by the analyst's framework of analysis, such that absolute objectivity cannot be presumed.[7]

TO BE OR NOT TO BE: AWAY FROM CYNICISM, TOWARD PROFESSIONAL NORMS

All of this has led to some cynicism about data gathering and empirical work in the social studies. One might chafe at going through the motions of gathering a data set and statistically analyzing it, if this process involves such a long chain of arbitrary assumptions that nearly any conclusion could be supported by any data. If we cannot get far enough outside our own biases to test any hypothesis, we can hardly claim to infer anything. In fact, one might claim that the process of using fancy mathematical techniques tends to give a scientific authority to claims that are, ultimately, unchallengeable precommitments.

Yet if we may invoke the analogy between the social sciences and detective work, this cynical attitude would be like excluding careful forensic work because the crime is not repeatable in a controlled environment and "lawyers can prove anything they want to." This attitude is built on a failure to distinguish between claims that can be supported through controlled experimentation and claims that cannot cite such solid foundations. The latter category, including much of the terrain of the social sciences, must be evaluated by considering the reasonableness of the case that is presented.

Empirical results in the social sciences should be part of a reasonable case. Crime lab results, like statistical results in the social sciences, are not conclusive in isolation. But this has not kept the criminal justice system from developing careful norms for the admissibility of lab work, to limit the number of hypotheses deemed reasonable. We really could not live in a world where "justice" became the unquestionable assertion of the loudest voices, and we should not let inquiry in the social sciences move in this direction either.[8]

So, we argue that the social sciences are in need of a set of norms to govern their basic measurement, modeling, and empirical activities. These norms should govern the admissibility of data, the development of statistical models that characterize these data, the lengths to which one may go to avoid falsification of a hypothesis, and the credibility assigned to various statistical results and tests of hypotheses.

Before pursuing this agenda, we should restate that some of these problems of the social sciences are differences of degree, not of kind, from the natural sciences. The history of scientific work is filled with examples of breakthroughs that resulted when someone decided that the available data were being misframed or the wrong variables were being controlled. Copernicus's view of the solar system and Einstein's revolution in physics are common examples. Yet the precommitments necessary to engage in experimental natural science often seem to be of a less ultimate variety, involving more humble claims than those involving human or social data. One's basic philosophy of life and human nature seems less frequently at issue; the subject matter seems less prone to the measurement problems involved with human subjects; and the possibility of conducting controlled experiments does often discipline the definitions, theory, measurement techniques, and claims made by the natural scientist in a way that is often lacking in the social sciences.

So in the social sciences, as in courts of law and some nonexperimental natural sciences, the restraint and discipline that is lost owing to the nature of the subject and data must be reimposed in the form of professional norms. It usually cannot be imposed by the construction of a control group.

Social science is a cultural event; its order is created by a combination of both the discipline imposed by external reality and the choices of norms made by practitioners.

▓ TOWARD NORMS FOR
THE DEVELOPMENT OF MODELS

How are we to proceed? Recall that our most severe problems stem from the twin realities of nonexperimental data and extremely complex situations. Use of the commonplace statistical tools of the social sciences is one way of trying to construct an artificial, simplified, abstracted "control group" from nonexperimental data. When Laura wants to measure a demand curve, she cannot put a panel of buyers through a recession, then back through a bull market, and watch how they respond to price changes differently in the two situations. But she can gather data on price and sales in prosperous times and recessions, then try to reconstruct the results that a controlled experiment would have generated. This is how the social sciences typically work out the problems generated by complex, nonexperimental situations. We want to identify norms that will facilitate this process.

Like natural scientists, social scientists begin by presuming or "reasonably believing" that the most influential factors in the situation under study have been identified so that the model is "well specified." The deleted, unmodeled disturbing influences are believed to be, on average, random and unpredictable; they usually enter the model, if at all, as a random (or "stochastic") error term in a regression equation. They may have an influence, but it is presumed to be small and, on average, of no account.

For this presumption about our model to be reasonable, we must know a great deal of specific information about the situation being modeled. How can one make a reasonable model, a confident exclusion of minor influences and inclusion of more important factors, without this background? Just as the detective must visit the crime scene, conduct interviews, be in the homes of suspects, and always be alert for the unsuspected small clue that opens up an entirely different way of framing the information, so a social scientist must really know the many details surrounding the issue under study. Our textbooks teach us differently. They generally give terse problems to be mechanically solved, using data that are easily accessible but often a distant proxy for the actual variable that should appear in the theory. The emphasis is on mastery of a technique that appears to generate significance even when separated from knowledge of the world under study. We train people to be fingerprint-lifting technicians, not detectives.

This establishes our first methodological norm for this chapter:

> *For each situation under analysis, practitioners benefit from a detailed understanding of the situation, from different disciplinary perspectives when possible, before the problem is modeled.*

Careful model specification is not the only casualty when social scientists fail to carefully study the situations they model. The reward system in the social sciences, for practitioners and students, penalizes broad attention to detail and as a result encourages an odd sense of what work is worthwhile.[9] The ethical implication is that social science students and practitioners often jump too quickly to quantification and statistical analyses, even if the characteristics under study cannot be measured appropriately on an interval, ratio, or absolute scale. It is tempting to replace "even if" in the last sentence with "especially if," because there is a great deal of peer pressure to be novel, to find a ground-breaking result, when there may be every good reason that this particular result has not yet been reported in the literature.

This motivates our second norm:

> *Practitioners should learn what is important enough to measure before trying to measure it, then decide which of the five measurement scales[10] is appropriate. One must then live within the bounds imposed by the characteristics of that measurement scale.*

If these first two norms were scrupulously observed in the teaching and practice of formal methods in the social sciences, we expect there would be a significant change in the fabric of these disciplines.

▓ FROM MODEL SPECIFICATION TO INFERENCE: NONEXPERIMENTAL DATA AND "RANDOM ERROR"

Say (as we always initially presume) that careful attention to the specifics of the situation has resulted in a correct specification of the model and that the relevant variables have been properly measured. Then we refer to the influences of the unspecified, excluded potential variables as the random error term. This error term is, in effect, a way to formally model the abstractions and approximations that occur when we put a theory into a form that can be tested.

This modeling-and-measurement strategy we are describing allows us to make a start in the world and is itself a partially testable starting point, but only if we carefully identify what we mean by random error when using nonexperimental data.

With the standard textbook presentation of statistical methods, based on the presumption of scientifically controlled and repeatable experiments, a person hopes to actually measure uncertainty and narrow it by sampling repeatedly from a stable population. In this classical case, probabilities mean the relative frequencies with which events occur after repeated sampling.

Because social scientists usually cannot repeat events under the same conditions, they are modeling the "unsameness" of events by including the possibility of random white noise. This is justified by the belief that we have organized the variables (i.e., specified the model) so that this noise (unspecified influences and approximations) has, on average, no influence on the relationships among the variables we are studying.

For example, a researcher may be interested in the effect of schooling and neighborhood income on violent crime. After considering her options, she uses census tract data from 10 large cities to measure average incomes, number of homicides, and proportion of the tract holding a high school diploma. She estimates the equation

$$\text{Homicide rate} = b_1 + b_2 \,(\text{Income}) + b_3 \,(\text{Proportion graduated}) + e.$$

Here the b_is are the coefficients to be estimated and e is the random error term.

Now what exactly does "random" mean when applied to the nonexperimental data of this example?[11] The data are not the result of a repeatable random draw from a stable population. Remember, we are not really involved in experiments. From what "population" were the data drawn for this month's number of homicides? Here the "sample" *is* the population, and the current situation will not be repeated in a future month, from which another random sample might be drawn. In fact, by the time the data are generated the events in question *already* have occurred. So, in what sense can we talk about their "relative frequency"?

An event does not have much frequency if we can be certain that it will only happen once, in the past.

Therefore, our actual practice implies that we are giving nonclassical meanings to the words "probabilities" and "randomness," due to our dependence on nonexperimental data. Statistical methods are being used not only to summarize data but also to simulate the control groups and random sampling that are essential to scientific work. But this has implications for the way we should define "probability" and "random," as well as the way we should interpret hypothesis tests and confidence intervals. These tests and intervals also take on different meanings from those in classical statistics.

It is clear that we cannot mean the word "random" in a literal sense here.[12] "Random error" is being used as a metaphor; it is a way to model our ignorance. "Random" does not (as in classical statistics) refer only to observations and events; it is actually our *knowledge* of events, our model and measurement of them, which is random, influenced by errors and ignorance. We are modeling all of this as randomness. Our choices of which variables to exclude and which functional forms to use and how to measure proxies are all made subject to error, and these errors will create noise that knocks our observations away from the places our theory would predict they should be. The best we can hope for is that we will make these errors in a way that leaves the resulting noise nonsystematic, that is, not polluting our estimates of the coefficients in the model.

Hence, norm number three:

Random error terms convey information about the abstractions, approximations, ignorance, and measurement problems that are involved in the model we have constructed. The drawing of inferences should therefore involve a careful inspection of the residual errors between our data and our model.

It is all right, then, to speak metaphorically of the "chance" that a nonrepeatable social science event would be observed, or the "probability" that a parameter takes a particular value, *if* we are careful about the meanings of chance and probability. Classical statistics, using experimental data, yields the likelihood that we have correctly accepted or rejected a null hypothesis, but with nonexperimental data the null hypothesis itself has a "probability" or degree-of-belief attached to it. Probabilities here are degrees of warranted belief, not relative frequencies. Probabilities are indexes of the reasonableness-of-doubt that should be attached to our conclusions—conclusions that, as in court cases, generally cannot be proven or disproved but can be argued more or less persuasively. Probability is not a statement about physical events but an estimate of the level of believability, the relative weight of admissible evidence in the face of uncertainty and ignorance; it is an assessment of the likelihood of a particular conclusion, given a body of (imperfect) information.

Probabilities in the social sciences are therefore formal ways of translating degrees of reasonable belief into real numbers. These probability numbers then conform to several norms of measurement regarding a proper "probability measure"; for example, probabilities of all possible outcomes must sum to one.

This all amounts to a method for moving from an ordinal ranking to a ratio scale measurement of subjective degrees of belief. But this raises a serious problem for the use of classical probability theory in the social sciences: We have argued that ratio scales are only appropriate if one has a well worked out theory of the entity being measured, a "correspondence theorem" that justifies the claim that the entity in fact behaves like the real numbers. Do we have such a theory of "subjective degrees of belief"? Can we, for example, be confident that a result that bears a probability of .42 is actually "half as believable" as a result whose probability is .84? And is this confidence intersubjective—true for all reasonable observers of the events? We are not aware of any satisfactory correspondence theory for subjective degrees of belief.

INTERPRETING CLAIMS OF INFERENCE

How will this affect our interpretation of the standard tests of hypotheses? We have seen that the hypotheses of social science are probabilistic, such that definitive rejections of hypotheses are rare. So social scientists try to set some boundaries on the admissibility of evidence that will limit the ability to maintain an unlikely hypothesis.

These boundaries generally are stated in terms of probabilities or required levels of statistical significance: If the data generate a statistic that is far from that expected by a given hypothesis, we say that this "unlikely" test statistic justifies a small level of believability in the hypothesis. We regard the hypothesis as rejected, though we must in humility acknowledge that it actually may be true. Because we have just seen that such probabilities are measured on a ratio scale that is not strictly justified, the stated boundaries for significance and admissibility are, at best, a bit arbitrary. There is no magic "95% confidence level" that necessarily warrants or dismisses a result; the formal "degree of significance" of a result always must be held alongside the overall reasonableness of the entire model and its abstractions, knowledge about and specification of the situation, propriety of measurement scales for the variables, quality of data, and attendance to the residual errors from the modeling exercise.

We may summarize these ideas in norm number four:

"Probabilities" in the social and human sciences are degrees of warranted belief, not relative frequencies. But this means that the classical ratio scale of probabilities is not appropriate in the situations we are discussing. Therefore, the level of confidence in a result cannot be stated as a single number; significance involves a judgment about the reasonableness of the entire model and its data.

If the nature of the data in the social sciences requires that practitioners should think of themselves more as detectives than as natural scientists, what does this imply for the general topic of this book, the bounds of formal models in the social sciences? The question becomes not one of identifying types of problems for which formal methods are not appropriate and others for which they will yield the right answers. By themselves the methods never can be relied on to yield correct answers. Similar to the act of collecting footprints or bullet fragments, formal methods can clarify reality, or obscure it, or create an alternative virtual reality that misleads. It is still common sense, creativity, and discernment that must be invoked when a practitioner sits down to a problem.

Instead of asking when formal methods yield the right answer, we should ask when to put a high degree of confidence in the limited information we get from formal methods. When one has solid data, clear contestable predictions, few auxiliary hypotheses, and a nonsystematic error term, one can afford to be less skeptical. Before invoking statistical tests of hypotheses, we would do well to ask if we know the situation being modeled and if fair persons with similar knowledge would trust the general approach to the problem and the results obtained.

A digest of the main reasons for skepticism should help prepare us to constrain the limitations of formal methods. This motivates a fifth norm:

Levels of statistical significance are always somewhat arbitrary, but we should be especially skeptical in cases when (a) the social processes under study are extremely complex, with many auxiliary hypotheses complicating the primary hypotheses; (b) the entity being measured is not clearly definable, or there is a poorly developed theory of the entity and its relationship to the measurable variables, or the measurement instrument is not precise and reliable; (c) inappropriate measurement scales are used; (d) the statistical methods (and, when present, functional forms) employed are not consistent with the measurement scale; (e) the specification of the model and its functional form are not clearly justified by reference to the actual situation being modeled; (f) the error residuals are not observed and analyzed (e.g., some ANOVA and correlation studies); and (g) the quality of the data and reliability of the source are questionable. We should be particularly skeptical when the analyst does not fully disclose the relevant information on these topics. In fact, it should be a professional norm that the statement of one's results must, as a matter of habit, discuss these issues.

WHAT SIGNIFICANCE TESTS CANNOT TEST: SIGNIFICANCE

Every practitioner must adopt some norms and procedures for evaluating the significance of the results of empirical work. What exactly do the common standards, a significance test and that test's level of confidence, mean?

If we were dealing with experimental scientific data, probabilities would have the nature of relative frequencies. But we have argued that this is inappropriate for nonexperimental data. Thus, each decision in the investigative processes has been justified on a probabilistic, degree-of-reasonable-belief basis and might have been mistaken. As the process proceeds, the probability of error compounds, such that the stated levels of confidence may have no relation to the actual believability of the result; any significance claimed for the final result is actually presuming that all previous decisions were made without error. This so-called "pretest bias" problem in the social sciences disallows the classical interpretations of test statistics.[13]

There is no clear, canonical solution to this problem; practitioners must deal with it informally. It is a problem common to all detective work. A detective, judge, or jury can speak of a reasonable, judgmental, supported-but-subjective degree of belief but not of "rejecting innocence at a 5% level of confidence." But there are certain disciplines, guidelines, and norms that the empirical investigator may adopt, evidentiary and cross-examination rules if you will, to reduce the likelihood of falsely claiming reliability for any given result.

Several guidelines have been proposed for the social sciences.

1. Calculate the actual power of all tests, not just their confidence levels. ("Power" is the probability of appropriately rejecting the null hypothesis when it is, in fact, false. It is equal to one minus the probability of a Type II error, where Type II error is the mistake of wrongly retaining a false hypothesis.)[14] Unfortunately, this guideline assumes that all "pretest" decisions and errors are independent of each other. Nonexperimental data usually represent situations in which the alternative hypotheses are not independent but composite, and the relationships between various pretest decisions and errors are unknowable. Yet there may be some rules of thumb for deflating the routinely overblown claims of statistical significance.[15]

2. Informally incorporate the potential for pretest bias, by refusing to interpret one's work as if all decisions were made correctly. Beyond simple humility in stating one's findings, this hermeneutic of suspicion can be institutionalized. Investigators always should report the steps taken in arriving at the final result being presented, and these should arise out of a well-conceived search strategy. Readers then are able to evaluate the extent to which errors may have compounded in the process.

3. Exercise caution in the use of tests of statistical significance.

Significance tests have severe restrictions and difficult requirements for use in any research endeavor, and both the opportunities for and the actualities of misuse are great. . . . The conditions for the use of the tests . . . are not and cannot be met in most behavioral research.[16]

Roughly three-quarters of the contributors to the *American Economic Review* misuse the test of significance. They use it to persuade themselves that a variable is important. But the test can only affirm a likelihood of excessive skepticism in the face of errors arising from too small a sample. The test does *not* tell the economist whether a fitted coefficient is large or small in an economically significant sense. . . . Even under classical conditions the t-test is irrelevant much of the time.[17]

Measures of statistical significance offer little information about the actual scientific or theoretical importance, the *substantive* significance, of one's results.[18] Statistical significance is an index of how unusual it might be to observe the sample one has collected if the maintained hypothesis were exactly true. This tells us nothing about how close our result must be to a theoretical value to conclude that the theory is a success or failure nor how big a coefficient must be to be relevant and important. In large samples, an inconsequentially small difference still may be statistically significant; the relationship between size of difference and statistical significance of difference depends on sample size. But substantive significance and the degree of precision required of a study depend on the context and motivations for the study.[19] If we had a large enough sample to be absolutely certain of the coefficient's true value, we would still need to determine the practical, substantive significance of this value and the goodness of the hypothesis—the "so what?" questions—by appeal to some responsible human criterion.

> The usual test [of statistical significance] does not discuss standards. It gives them up in favor of irrelevant talk about the probability of a Type I error in view of the logic of random sampling. Most economists appear to have forgotten how narrow is the question that a statistical test of significance answers. . . . Though not to be scorned, it isn't much. It warns him about a certain narrow kind of foolishness.[20]

Empirical work therefore needs to discuss the substantive significance of the things it measures, the power of the tests it uses, and the many twists and turns through which the final results were achieved. This will involve analysts in the discussion of human values, and the discussion will overlap both statistical and decision science methodologies.[21] The empirical analyst must therefore regard inferences as contributory evidence, not as objective proof that removes the need for insight, common sense, and persuasion. Statistical inference can offer evidence but cannot supply the criteria by which it is admitted.

▦ NOTES

1. Subsections of the natural sciences are also somewhat "nonexperimental," such as astronomy, geology, and biology. Many of our conclusions will have relevance for parts of

these fields as well. And some subsections of the social sciences, as discussed in the previous two chapters, make claims to the generation of experimental data. We have made the case that, even in such instances, the social sciences face special difficulties in conducting experimental studies. For a review of the options for experimental social data, see Campbell and Stanley (1963) or Cook and Campbell (1979). We judge (along with Babbie, 1986) that experiments are generally appropriate only for limited, well-defined concepts and claims; that they usually succeed in small-group research settings; and that so-called "natural (i.e., nonlaboratory) experiments" involve the same problems we are discussing under nonexperimental data.

2. One might argue this is the case, for example, in some areas of psychology or experimental economics. See the previous note, along with Heckman and Smith (1995), and Burtless (1995).

3. For example, one often must choose which particular country, culture, time period, and length of period will be included in the study.

4. See Radelet (1981).

5. Radelet (1981). A similar example appears in Moore (1995, p. 160).

6. Radelet concluded that those accused of murdering whites are more likely to be indicted for first degree murder; he did not find clear support for the hypothesis that race of defendant is associated with probability of a first degree murder indictment nor with imposition of the death penalty.

7. The problem of irrefutability is further complicated by the practice of accepting observations, especially observations of dependent variables, as being stochastic, hovering around some expected value but observed with some error owing to mistakes in measurement or modeling. This opens a rather wide door toward irrefutability: How far away from a predicted expected value must an observation fall before we take it as evidence of a bad theory rather than a random disturbance? This problem is further amplified in the social sciences by the nonexperimental nature of the data: The experimental scientist is on firmer ground in claiming that the data were actually coincident with the model plus an error term, not generated by an entirely different specification.

8. There are limits to the courtroom analogy, especially for readers from the United States. One might say that the U.S. legal system is too adversarial and does less to disclose the truth than to reward the best rhetoric. Lawyers aim to present only one side of a case, whereas we argue that scientists must aim to present all sides as fairly as possible.

9. See, for example, Feige (1975) or Tullock (1959).

10. See Chapters 5 and 6 for a fuller development of the notion of measurement scales and the attributes and limits of the five options.

11. This section relies on the detailed discussion of the notion of "randomness" in nonexperimental settings in Darnell and Evans (1990, Chapter 1).

12. A standard definition of "simple random sampling," though misapplied to nonexperimental situations, is found, for example, in Anderson, Sweeney, and Williams (1993, p. 777): "A simple random sample of size n from a finite population of size N is a sample selected such that every possible sample of size n has the same probability of being selected." This obviously cannot be typical of the kinds of social data we have been discussing.

13. We have also argued that measurement theory indicates that ratio scales, such as probabilities, are strictly inappropriate for nonexperimental data in which probabilities index degrees of reasonable belief.

14. For example, the true probability for a test procedure will be the power of its pretest, which in turn has a power that depends on the Type II errors of all previous pretests.

15. See Lovell (1983).

16. Morrison and Henkel (1970, p. 310).

17. McCloskey (1985, p. 201). The article provides a brief review of the 70-year history of warnings about misuses of "significance" tests, all generally ignored by social science practitioners.

18. Medical studies speak of "clinical" significance when discussing these issues of substantive significance. A blood pressure decline of 1% may be statistically significant at the .05 level, but this change may not have any clinical significance—in practical terms, it may not matter.

19. In some cases one might model this idea by including in the model a loss function, an index of how much harm is caused by deviations of a result from its theoretical value. If there is a large range of findings for which there is a small cost of error, the substantive significance of the result will be different from when there is a small range for which there is a large cost of error. The relative size of the range and cost will depend on the context, and this cannot be assessed on statistical or technical grounds.

20. McCloskey (1985, p. 202).

21. See, for example, Arrow (1960, pp. 70-78).

EIGHT

Causality

We are now approaching the end of the information cycle. One important issue in the interpretation of information still needs to be discussed, causality. Starting from data, claims are frequently made that one factor caused another. Arguments about the legitimacy of such claims are perhaps as frequent.

Consider two controversial issues: the claim that smoking causes lung cancer and the claim that differences in IQ scores between African Americans and white Americans can be attributed largely to genetic factors. The social impact of these two issues is enormous. The smoking and lung cancer issue involves the health of millions of people plus potentially billions of dollars in liability for the tobacco industry. The genetic attribution of IQ differences has influenced the discussion of race relations in the United States and could affect the funding of many antipoverty programs. We need principles that can help us assess such claims about causation.

Causal analyses of social phenomena are eagerly sought. They have great explanatory power when they are available, and they have a significant impact on governmental, commercial, and service sector policy by indicating which interventions are likely to succeed. But as we have seen in other aspects of the use of data and models, the existence of high incentives introduces temptations to achieve benefits by short cuts. Our strategy in this chapter will be to

- clarify the meaning of the term *causal,*
- discuss how causality can be established,
- examine some common difficulties that arise when trying to establish causality for social phenomena, and
- look at some normative implications of the previous three steps.

We will conclude with a case study—the debate over whether the observed differences in IQ scores between African Americans and white Americans can be attributed largely to genetic factors.

THE MEANING OF CAUSALITY

A cause traditionally has been thought of as a variable that produces something and can be used to explain that something. Causality has been studied extensively since the time of Greek philosophers. Two important conceptions of causality given by Aristotle are still central to the discussion today. One is the notion of "efficient" cause—that by which some change is wrought. The other is the notion of "final" cause—the use or purpose for which a change is produced. Since roughly the 18th century, empirical science has focused on efficient causes and largely has dismissed consideration of final causes, primarily because the latter are not accessible to empirical analysis. Approaches that focus on final causes are called *teleological.* Thus, psychological explanations that focus on human intentionality and seek to interpret human motivations are teleological. Similarly, a Marxist interpretation of economics is teleological in that it sees history as moving toward a goal—the formation of a classless society. And certainly, theological explanations of human existence are teleological in that they start from an understanding of God's purposes. But, as we saw in Chapter 4, scientific explanations typically have not involved teleological elements—their domains are replicable phenomena that are deterministic or probabilistic, and such explanations are presented as laws possessing predictive power. Thus, physicists, biologists, experimental psychologists, and other empirical scientists largely have rejected teleological explanations.

We are not attempting to settle here the matter of which aspects of human behavior best can be explained teleologically and which best can be explained by invoking efficient causes. The matter is part of an ancient debate over free will versus determinism that has continued for thousands of years and shows no signs of resolution. Note, however, that these two types of explanations are not always mutually exclusive; they may complement each other and together provide for a richer understanding. Consider the following example. Suppose a physics teacher climbs onto a chair, planning to drop an object to demonstrate some aspect of gravity. But he slips and falls to the floor. His falling can be explained in physical terms—in terms of gravity and the water spilled on the chair, thereby reducing the coefficient of friction. Or it could be explained teleologically, in terms of his profession as a physics teacher, what the previous experiment in which the water had spilled was supposed to demonstrate, and why he was climbing onto the chair. The two explanations serve different purposes. Teleological explanations are necessarily interpretive because they answer "why" questions; causal explanations (in the Aristotelian sense of "efficient" cause) are deterministic or probabilistic because they answer "how" questions. Because (efficient) causal claims are often based on data and models, whereas teleological explanations are typically not (inasmuch as they involve unobservables, such as intentionality), our focus for the rest of this chapter will be on efficient causality; in fact, we shall drop the word "efficient" and simply refer to "causality."

The concept of causality has many subtle and elusive features; in fact it has been called a "notorious philosophical tar pit."[1] We are going to risk a very brief history of the notion as it has been treated in the social sciences. Our treatment will oversimplify a complex subject, but it will provide us a means to introduce some major concepts and will set a context for our subsequent discussion of the contemporary understanding of causality.

Perhaps the modern philosopher most associated with the contemporary concept of causality is David Hume (1711-1776). Prior to the rise of empiricism, causality was largely seen in terms of "power," that is, a cause was something that had the power to assure certain consequences. Hume's notion was that cause and effect are merely changes that are "constantly conjoined." Thus, Hume dropped the notion of power and any other necessary connection between cause and effect. The relationship between cause and effect is simply a matter of habits of expectation we develop from observing the cause and effect together. Another significant figure is

Auguste Comte (1798-1857), the founder of positivism. Comte described each branch of human knowledge as proceeding through three distinct stages, the theological (which he also called fictitious), the metaphysical (or abstract), and the scientific (or positive). Comte explicitly rejected teleological explanations and any notion of final causes. He sought scientific laws and causal explanations for the social sciences analogous to those found in the natural sciences.

John Stuart Mill (1806-1873) spoke of the "ascent to science." Mill's notion was that knowledge development should proceed by scientific induction based on experience rather than from theology. Mill recognized that induction cannot provide a proof of causality, but he did not regard this as problematic.[2]

> [If] the number of instances in which a coincidence is observed, over and above that which would arise on the average from the mere concurrence of chances, be such that so great an amount of coincidences from accident alone would be an extremely uncommon event; we have reason to conclude that the coincidence is the effect of causation, and may be received (subject to correction from further experience) as an empirical law. Further than this, in point of precision, we cannot go; nor, in most cases, is greater precision required, for the solution of any practical doubt. (p. 37)

Mill also removed a distinction common at the time between *conditions* and *causes*. For instance, suppose a child slips on an icy sidewalk and breaks her arm. Was the cause of the fall the ice? Or the smooth soled boots she was wearing? Or the weather, the social custom of building sidewalks, the phone call from her friend inviting her to come over to play, or the decision by the principal to close the school that day and so forth. Mill responded to this sort of complexity as follows.[3] "The cause, then, philosophically speaking, is the sum of the conditions, positive and negative taken together; the whole of the contingencies of every description, which being realized, the consequent invariably follows" (p. 31). To Mill, the cause of a phenomenon is the total assemblage of its conditions. Also, Mill largely accepted Hume's notion of causality as invariant sequence. Thus, causality is established, according to Mill, by observing *concomitant variation,* or as we would call it today, correlation. Mill also believed that because of the complexity of human affairs, scientific laws in the social sciences would have to take a different form than they do in the natural sciences—as *approximate generalizations* or *approximate tendencies*.

Lambert Adolphe Quetelet (1796-1874) spoke of producing a "social physics" and introduced the notion of *l'homme moyen* or the average man. In his view, individuals vary greatly, but these variations are largely effaced at the level of the aggregate statistical observation. It is at this level that causal laws for the social sciences should be sought. He measured the chests of 5,378 Scottish recruits to the British army and observed that the measurements were distributed in a bell curve pattern. He regarded such a regular pattern as evidence of a law for human development. Durkheim, whose research on suicide we examined in Chapter 5, also looked for laws in aggregates. He adopted Mill's notion of causality as concomitant variation but insisted that such variations must not be accidental.

And one last important figure is Karl Pearson (1857-1936), a giant in the history of statistics. Pearson regarded the task of finding the true determining cause of a phenomenon as a hopeless undertaking, whereas the establishment of correlation was "of first class practical importance" and fully achievable.[4] In fact, Pearson regarded correlation as an adequate substitute for the concept of cause.

In summary, then, the tendency of 18th to early 20th-century philosophers and social scientists was to move toward a concept of causality that focused on aggregates rather than individuals. It was based in the empirical, natural science model but recognized that in the social sciences causality had to be seen as tendencies rather than precise predictions. It also tended to conflate the notions of correlation and causation.

Contemporary thinking in the social sciences about causality has some notably different features from the ideas advanced by such scholars as Mill and Pearson. We will summarize a few features that are especially relevant to our concern with norms for evaluating causal claims.

The first feature is a clear distinction between correlation and causality. For instance, if one were to carefully measure the ambient light outdoors hourly during a 12-hour period from midnight to noon on some day, one would find a strong positive correlation between time and light. But the change in time has not caused the change in light, nor vice versa. Such a correlation is called *spurious*. This is the notion Durkheim attempted to express in saying that correlations must not be accidental if they are to imply causality. Thus, in the view of many contemporary scholars, a claim of causality must not only demonstrate correlation but must also provide an explanation of a *mechanism* by which the cause produces the effect. "Mechanism" in this sense means an algorithmic process that explains how the causative agent is translated into the outcome. We will address this important notion in more detail later.

Another contemporary emphasis is on the avoidance of long causal chains. Thus, if one asks what caused a certain group of people to emigrate from Europe to America, one can describe the (complex) situation in Europe at the time. But then, one can ask what caused those conditions in Europe and another set of (also complex) causes could be advanced. Pursuing this pattern of argument leads to an ever lengthening causal chain, in which the causal relationship between remote events and current ones becomes ever more tenuous. The contemporary focus is on immediate causes and hence on very short causal chains.

A third emphasis is a distinction between necessary and sufficient conditions for causality. A necessary condition is one that must be present for an event to occur. Its presence does not guarantee occurrence but its absence guarantees nonoccurrence. A sufficient condition is one that guarantees that the event will occur whenever it is present. But the event still may occur in its absence. An ideal outcome of a scientific investigation would be a set of conditions that are simultaneously necessary and sufficient for an event. This would truly explain the event.

The hope of finding necessary and sufficient causal conditions is more of a regulating ideal than a realistic goal, however. Whereas there are many theorems in mathematical social science that establish necessary and sufficient conditions for some abstract condition, the authors of this book are not aware of a single situation in the social sciences in which such a set of necessary and sufficient causal conditions have been found for an empirically observable phenomenon. Several critics also have pointed out a weakness in the notion that causality can be broken down into the two concepts of necessary and sufficient conditions for causality. Suppose a set of conditions A is both necessary and sufficient for an event B. Then the two events are logically equivalent—neither can occur without the other and if either occurs, so must the other. Thus, B also is necessary and sufficient for A. If "causation" were fully explained by listing necessary and sufficient conditions, B could be regarded as causal for A and A also could be thought of as causal for B. Thus the notions of necessary and sufficient conditions for causality are helpful but lack the essential feature that causes must precede effects.

A fourth contemporary emphasis is the notion of *probabilistic causality*. This notion of causality can be formulated precisely using conditional probability: A is regarded as causal of B if knowing that A occurred changes our estimate of the probability that B will occur. Thus, this formulation allows for both negative and positive causal effects.[5] Note, however, that this definition of probabilistic causation still conflates correlation and causation: Knowing that A occurred indeed may change our estimate of the likelihood that B will occur even if the connection between A and B is entirely spurious. We shall see that correlation and causation can be distinguished while still maintaining a concept of probabilistic causality.

Finally, some philosophers have suggested that certain events, such as changes in states of elementary particles and some human actions, may occur without causes. But whether this is true is an open question.

Having reviewed the concept of "cause," we are now in a position to address the critical question: (How) can we know the cause of anything?

HOW TO ESTABLISH CAUSALITY

The classic scientific technique for establishing causality is the controlled experiment. Thus, if one wants to determine whether a particular type of plant will grow better with nutrient Z added to its fertilizer, one can select many plants, maintain the light, water, soil, and other fertilizer nutrients at a constant level, and change only the levels of nutrient Z. Differences in growth then are attributable to the one nutrient. Of course, the circumstances of the different plants are never quite identical—the individual plants are not the same for one thing, and some differences in watering, exposure to sunlight and so forth are inevitable. But as long as the plants receiving the different treatments are genetically similar, many individual plants are treated, and we assign plants randomly to the different treatments, systematic differences in treatment or genetic makeup are unlikely. Hence, we regard the experiment as sufficiently well controlled to justify the claim that growth differences are caused by the nutrient Z.

Such careful controls are difficult to achieve when studying human beings.[6] Nevertheless, randomization often can be approximated even when participants are not randomly assigned to groups (because the groups typically are intact). If sample sizes are large enough and subjects are chosen randomly enough that no systematic sources of bias creep in, then results of such quasi-experiments also can be used to justify claims of causality. For instance, if one were investigating the relationship between smoking and health, participants could not be randomly assigned as smokers or nonsmokers. Nevertheless, if enough smokers are randomly chosen and enough nonsmokers are randomly chosen, one hopes that all differences between the groups except the smoking factor have been reduced to insignificance. Of course, quasi-experimental results are never quite as convincing as experimental results because typically there are many variables changing simultaneously and many ways that systematic bias can enter inadvertently.

Because of these potential problems, Paul Lazarsfeld suggested three criteria for establishing a claim that variable X is causally related to variable Y. These criteria are now widely used.[7]

- The cause must precede the effect in time.
- The two variables must be empirically correlated.
- The correlation between the two variables cannot be explained by the existence of a third variable that influences both of them.

Whereas these principles seem obvious, their application can be subtle. For instance, suppose one wants to test a claim that authoritarianism causes prejudice. Both factors exist continuously in time and there is no easy way to tell which came first. So the first criterion is very hard to apply. As long as X and Y can be measured appropriately and appropriate data can be gathered, the second is a technical matter and not usually problematic. Nevertheless, the third can be problematic; a researcher may have searched in vain for a third factor influencing both variables, but one still may exist.

Clearly, controlled experiments, such as our plant growth example, satisfy Lazarsfeld's criteria. Careful quasi-experiments also can meet them. But Lazarsfeld was trying to go beyond these situations to show how causality can be established even in situations in which neither experiments nor quasi-experiments are available. It seems to us that although Lazarsfeld's criteria are helpful, they are insufficient to establish causality in such situations. Lazarsfeld's criteria do help us identify spurious correlations, but they neglect a deeper problem: Our attributions of causality are highly dependent on the conceptual framework we bring to our analysis. Hence, understandings of "cause" are never final. We will illustrate this point with a famous example in the history of social research.

William Farr (1807-1883) was trained as a physician and served for many years as Superintendent of the British Statistical Department. He made major contributions to the advance of epidemiology, through the use of statistics. One of his pioneering works was a study of a cholera outbreak in England.[8] Farr began with a distinction between "healthy counties" and "unhealthy counties" as the causal agent. But after more research he adopted a notion of "polluted water" as the causal agent. Note how substantial a change this was: from the relatively vague notions of healthy and unhealthy counties, he narrowed the source of the illness to the water supply. In fact, the triumph of Farr's work was that when use of the suspect water supplies was halted, the cholera outbreak abruptly ceased.

From our vantage point today, we regard Farr's work as naive. We see the causal agent as a cholera bacillus that lived in the water. But if we return to Lazarsfeld's criteria, we can see that the "polluted water" explanation satisfies all three criteria as does the bacillus explanation.

1. The water was polluted before the disease was contracted, because presumably it was drinking the water that communicated the disease.
2. The presence of the polluted water and the incidence of the disease are correlated.
3. No separate variable causing both the pollution in the water and the disease can be identified.

Although one is tempted to identify the presence of cholera bacilli as such a variable, the microorganisms do not *cause* the water to be polluted. The presence of bacilli does not precede the pollution, but the bacilli and the pollution occur simultaneously. Rather the identification of microorganisms as the cause of the cholera represents *a sharpening of the concept* of pollution. That is, the word *polluted* in this context means "containing cholera bacilli"—there is no meaningful way to define *polluted* that would enable one to identify the bacilli as the cause of the pollution.

If one sought a cause for the pollution, one would need an agent that preceded the pollution, such as nearby latrines. In fact, Farr had the right cause of the cholera outbreak. He just did not understand it as clearly as we do today and his explanation did not provide a way to decide if a particular water source was polluted until it had already sickened some people. Lazarsfeld's criteria *per se* cannot help with this kind of refinement of understanding and applying them may leave us with an inadequate understanding of the causes of a phenomenon.

"Microbes in the water" seems a better causal explanation than "polluted water" for two reasons: Water samples and a microscope provide a precise way to measure which water is polluted (in the relevant way), and the microbes provide us a mechanism for understanding how the disease is communicated and how it acts on our bodies. "Mechanism" is a critical point in many contemporary understandings of causality. As expressed by Stephen Turner, "The difference between Farr's cruder category of 'polluted water' and present causal categories is that a set of mechanisms has been specified that corresponds to present categories."[9]

It may be that 100 years from now people will regard our explanation in terms of a cholera bacillus as nearly as naive as Farr's concept of polluted water. That is, once a mechanism has been introduced as a category, it begs for further study to confirm and refine it. Thus, we can see our answer to our question of how causality can be established: A claim of causality requires that Lazarsfeld's criteria be met *and* a convincing mechanism described. But we also can see another critically important point. A claim of causality is never final; subsequent refinements in understanding may result in such a claim being viewed as naive or perhaps only a partial explanation.

As a second illustration of the importance of mechanism, consider the relationship between tobacco smoking and health. This is perhaps the single most-studied application of statistics. That tobacco smoking is correlated with the occurrence of many diseases in human beings has been known for years. But representatives of the tobacco industry still argue that causality has not been proven; they argue that the correlation could be spurious. Many studies examining this issue from many different directions have been conducted; Lazarsfeld's criteria have been abundantly met many times. In fact, smoking proved to be correlated with so many ailments that some outstanding statisticians concluded in the late 1950s and early 1960s that the studies must have been in error. But when it was demonstrated by controlled experiments that tobacco smoke damaged the capillaries in dogs and that similar lesions were found in human smokers, a mechanism was provided that explained the multitude of different health problems. Since that study, few statisticians or medical personnel doubt the pervasive harmful effects of smoking tobacco. But it took the explication of a mechanism to make the causal claim persuasive.[10]

In a way, we have not progressed past the insights of Hume and Mill. We still do not have a means to prove causality in any final sense. Rather, a claim of causality is fundamentally interpretative. Its credibility depends on its presentation of a mechanism that substantial numbers of people find compelling. At this point, it is not hard to see why Pearson wanted to replace causality with correlation. A claim of causality in terms of mechanism has an unavoidable nonempirical dimension. For instance, Patrick Suppes writes,[11]

> In recent years, mechanisms whose properties are not fully characterized are referred to as black boxes, especially in communication and information science. Back of this concept of a black box is a fundamental message about causal mechanisms which represents perhaps the most important philosophical separation between the classical tradition of Aristotle, Descartes, and Kant on the one hand, and the modern temperament on the other . . . [namely that] a grasp of mechanisms that are, in any final sense, ultimate is not to be achieved. . . . The analysis of causes and their identification must always be relative to a conceptual framework, and there is no successful line of argument apparently that can show that a particular conceptual framework represents some ultimate and correct view about the structure of the world. From the standpoint of either scientific investigation or philosophical analysis it can fairly be said that one man's mechanism is another man's black box. I mean by this that the mechanisms postulated and used by one generation are mechanisms that are to be explained and understood themselves in terms of more primitive mechanisms by the next generation. (pp. 90-91)

Even today we encounter attempts to establish causality while avoiding interpretation.[12] Most often these involve the notion of conditional probability. But when looked at closely, they typically redefine causality by conflating it with correlation.

SOME DIFFICULTIES IN ESTABLISHING CAUSALITY

Let's consider an example. Suppose a male dealer of American-made luxury cars wants to increase sales. He judges that he has a good product for the price and wants to target his advertising toward his most likely customers. That is, he wants to identify the causal variables that influence a person to buy one of his cars. He lists every variable he can think of that conceivably might have a significant effect on an individual's propensity to buy an American-made luxury car: age, income, attitude toward American-made automobiles, social status, type of employment, previous purchase history, savings, investments, and political affiliation.

We can now begin to see some difficulties faced in causal analysis.

- None of these variables is causally necessary, except attitude toward American-made luxury cars, and the whole set is probably not sufficient.

- All of them are probabilistically causal, that is, the best one can hope for is such information as "40% of people with income level x buy American-made luxury cars." No basis is provided for predicting precisely what any particular individual will do.

- One variable, social status, is hard to define precisely and hence hard to measure.

- Some, such as savings and investments, may be inaccessible to the automobile dealer.

- The whole process, to this point, is unsupported by data. It also depends on the categories the automobile dealer uses for analyzing his customer's motives.

But let's suppose our dealer decides to proceed despite these difficulties. First, he drops the unavailable variables and aims to see how much predictability he can get just from the variables that are available. Second, he decides to drop social status; not only is it hard to define but it would very likely end up being replaced by proxies anyway, and the likely proxies already have been listed.

Next he sets up a "causal diagram," a graphic representation of all of the variables with arrows drawn to show which ones could causally influence which others. (See Figure 8.1.)

Note another aspect of causal analysis: the assumptions about how variables influence each other are based partly on Lazarsfeld's first criterion (later cannot cause earlier) and partly on a complex combination of previous experience and linguistic categories that we could call intuition.

The particular causal diagram in Figure 8.1 has some features that make causal analysis in this problem easier than in many problems. First, there are no significant two-way influences. Second, there are no "feedback loops"—cases in which variable A influences variable B, but the result of the influence of A on B subsequently returns to influence A. Thus, Figure 8.1 can be redrawn as in Figure 8.2, in which it becomes clear that age is a "prior" variable and propensity to buy is the "consequent" variable.

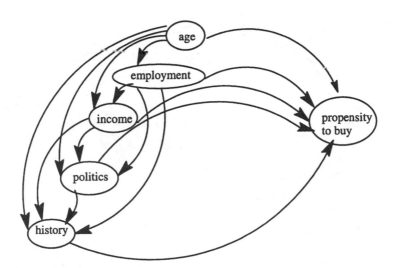

Figure 8.1. Causal diagram for automobile sales example.

Some additional technical difficulties can be seen at this point. A decision has to be made about what data to gather and how to gather them. Some of the variables are numerical (age, income) and some are categorical (political affiliation, employment type, history). Statistical tools are based on the assumption of random sampling, yet obtaining data from a random sample in this situation is hard to do.

But let's make the generous assumption that these problems have been solved satisfactorily. Our car dealer has a large collection of randomly selected data from his geographical area, including values for each of the variables listed in Figure 8.2. And let's make the very reasonable assumption that after statistical analysis, every variable yields a significant positive correlation with propensity to buy. (For example, suppose the sample is partitioned into cohorts of similarly aged persons. Those aged 16-25 might be one cohort, 26-35 another cohort, and so forth. In assuming a positive correlation, we are assuming that the proportion of people in each cohort that buy American-made luxury cars tends to increase as age increases.) Because all of the explanatory variables are correlated with sales, how do we decide which of these correlations involve causal relationships and which are spurious? To avoid getting bogged down in technical details, we will simply point out that there are statistical techniques that allow an analyst to sort out how much of each correlation is due to the direct relationship and how much to the indirect relationships.[13] Let's suppose

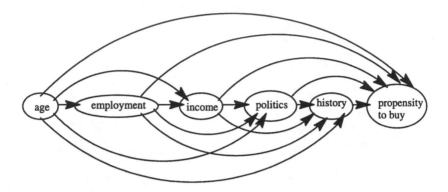

Figure 8.2. Figure 8.1 redrawn to show priority.

this has been done. Say that income and purchase history turn out to be significant influences, but age is only a minor influence. Say the correlations with employment type and political affiliation turn out to be spurious.

It seems that our car dealer has achieved his purpose. He should target high-income people and people who have previously purchased an American-made luxury car. He also may want to target older people. But is the conclusion of causality here a valid one? Or is our car dealer simply at the same point Farr was when he offered polluted water as the causal explanation for the cholera outbreak? Again we can see the necessity of mechanism. Our dealer has no way to answer the question of validity; as we mentioned earlier, causal explanations are never final. It is not hard to concoct fairly compelling explanations for how these variables are causal. But there is no guarantee that someone who conducts a similar study with different categories might not come up with stronger correlations and more convincing explanations. Yet, it is important to note that causal explanations may be quite helpful even if they are subsequently seen to be naive. The application of Farr's concept, by eliminating polluted water, stopped the cholera outbreak. And our car dealer will likely improve his sales with his targeted advertising.

Our example has been fairly simple. Sometimes feedback loops do in fact arise. In this case causal analysis is much more difficult. Sometimes causes seem to exist in a kind of symbiotic relationship, that is, two or more must be present for the effect to occur. Testing each individually leads to the (invalid) conclusion that they are not causal. In other studies, it is impossible for researchers to protect from contamination. For example, the study of an educational innovation may be discussed outside of the setting where it takes place. Thus, follow-up studies have been influenced by the reputation of the first study. And many questions we would like to ask involve counterfactuals, that is, questions of the form "Suppose such and such a condition hadn't been present. What would have happened?" Such questions are ultimately unanswerable. We can try to simulate the situation without the condition in question but frequently enough other variables have changed to make the simulation an inadequate substitute for the original situation.

In summary, then, empirical and methodological techniques exist that are extremely helpful in identifying causal variables. But such techniques are limited and nonempirical factors are unavoidable. Such factors enter at the beginning—in the identification of likely causes—and at the end, in the development of a convincing mechanism as explanation of a possible causal relationship.

SOME IMPLICATIONS

What methodological norms can we identify that are applicable to causal analysis? The most obvious one, but one that frequently is ignored, is that correlation does not equal causality. This principle is a standard topic in elementary statistics courses, yet still is often forgotten. A second norm is closely related to it: Causal attributions always involve an interpretation that is relative to the categories and understandings of mechanism available when the study is written. Thus, they never can be claimed with certainty, and fully algorithmic approaches to establishing causality are never going to work.

Another norm that seems obvious, but is easily ignored, is that probabilistically causal arguments (including virtually all causal arguments involving human information) cannot be applied to individuals. For instance, suppose poverty is probabilistically causal for some social problem. Enabling an *individual* to get out of poverty does not guarantee that the social problem related to poverty will be alleviated for that individual, although averaged over many individuals an improvement should be seen.

And last, causal inferences are based on assumptions, such as replicability and the existence of laws. As such they indeed may provide useful analyses of deterministic and probabilistic aspects of situations. But other aspects (such as those dependent on human intentionality) require a different methodology to be understood.

Also, we again see the necessity of contextual norms for decision making: Even if one understands the causal agents in a situation, intervention requires principles that tell us what a desirable outcome would be and that justify an intervention to achieve it. And even if a decision to intervene is justified, because of the probabilistic nature of causality, a good decision does not guarantee a good outcome. That is, a decision must be based on what is likely to happen. But if an unlikely event occurs a (good) decision can yield poor results.

Last, a final norm is the need for humility in the face of the enormous complexity of social phenomena and the difficulties in identifying causes.

A CASE STUDY

Let's consider the claim advanced by several writers, including Richard Herrnstein and Charles Murray in *The Bell Curve,* that differences in IQ scores between American blacks and American whites are caused by genetic factors. Although much of *The Bell Curve* has been discredited, we have chosen to analyze it here for two reasons: the importance of the issues it raises and the clarity with which it illustrates improper attributions of causality. More precisely, Herrnstein and Murray's claim is "that IQ is substantially inheritable, somewhere between 40 and 80 percent, meaning that much of the observed variation in IQ is genetic."[14] If we look first at Lazarsfeld's three criteria, we immediately observe a problem with the second criterion—that for one variable to be a cause of another, they must at least be correlated. But there is no correlation between genetics and IQ scores; there is no presently known way to measure a genetic factor that has been shown to be correlated with IQ. In fact, what is correlated with IQ is self-reported race. Race also satisfies Lazarsfeld's first criteria—it precedes IQ testing in time—and his third one—there is no known third variable that causes both race and IQ scores.[15] Thus "genetics" is being used by Herrnstein and Murray in a confused way. It is not clear whether genetics is presented as a factor that might be measured precisely enough to establish a correlation, or whether it serves as a mechanism that explains the causal attribution of the difference in IQ scores to self-reported race.

The first of these two possibilities is untestable at present. Some studies of identical twins suggest that there may be inheritable factors in IQ, although such studies are not as yet regarded as conclusive. But no one has identified which genes are responsible for intelligence or to identify any other measurable genetic factor that is correlated with IQ. So the only way to clarify Herrnstein and Murray's claim (at least within the framework of our present knowledge) is to say that they are asserting that race is the causal factor and genetics is the mechanism. Thus, the critical question we need to ask is whether genetics is a compelling mechanism for explaining these differences. Herrnstein and Murray justify their assertion that it is compelling by making several claims. We will simply list these claims, then critique them later.

An Environmental Explanation Is Implausible. They say that if one makes the estimate that IQ is 60% heritable, the

> observed ethnic differences in IQ could be explained solely by the environment if the mean environment of whites is 1.58 standard deviations better than the mean environment of blacks. . . . The average environment of blacks would have to be at the 6th percentile of the distribution of environments among whites. . . . Environmental differences of this magnitude and pattern are implausible.[16]

A Genetic Explanation Is Plausible Because Profile Differences in Intellectual Capacities Between Races Has Been Demonstrated. They justify this claim by several studies that suggested differences between Asians and whites on verbal and visuospatial abilities and on tests that show that blacks tend to do more poorly on *g* loaded tests. (For more information on *g*, see the case study on measuring intelligence at the end of Chapter 6.)

g Is Correlated With Neurological Processing Time, and Whites Process Faster Than Blacks.[17] This particular point suggests a possible explanation for intelligence differences among people—that intelligence is a function of neurological processing time.

A Study of Differences Between Adopted Children Reveals Racial Differences.[18]

> Just over 100 families with adopted children of white, black, and mixed racial ancestry are being studied in an ongoing analysis of the effects of being raised by white adopting parents of middle or higher social status.

At about age 7,

The mean IQs were 117 for the biological children of white parents, 112 for the white adoptive children, 109 for the adopted children with one black and one white or Asian parent, and 97 for the adopted children with two black parents.

A decade later,

The new ordering of IQ means was 109 for the biological children of white parents, 106 for the white adoptive children, 99 for the adopted children with one black parent, and 89 for the adopted children with two black parents. (p. 309)

IQ Scores of African Blacks Are Substantially Lower Than Scores of American Blacks. Eleven studies were assembled by Richard Lynn in 1991. He[19]

estimated the median black African IQ to be 75, approximately 1.7 standard deviations below the U.S. population average. . . . The IQ of "colored" students in South Africa—of mixed racial background—has been found to be similar to that of American blacks. (p. 289)

The most compelling way to show that a purported causal mechanism is not convincing is to present another mechanism that explains the observations as well or better. Note here a very important point. As critics of Herrnstein and Murray's assertion of a genetic explanation, we do not need to *prove* that any particular alternate explanation is correct. It is only necessary to present a *possible* alternative explanation that is as compelling as theirs. That is, Herrnstein and Murray assert that race is the causal factor in the IQ score differences. But race has many aspects—environmental and cultural as well as genetic. A mechanism is simply a convincing explanation of how race could have produced the differences in scores. Thus, their claim that genetic differences have been convincingly shown to be the mechanism is invalidated if an alternate explanation as compelling as genetics is brought forward, even if it has not yet been proven.

It seems to us that there is such an alternate explanation of the black-white differences in measured IQ, namely, cultural differences in prenatal and early childhood experiences.[20] This hypothesis becomes particularly compelling when seen in light of an animal study of brain growth.[21] In this study, sets of newly born laboratory rats were assigned to one of three different environments: remaining in a cage with the rat colony, an enriched cage, or an impoverished cage. After living in these environments from 4 to 10 weeks, the rats were sacrificed and autopsies performed on them. It was found that the rats that had lived in the enriched environment had significantly heavier and thicker cerebral cortices. The cerebral cortex is the part of the brain responsible for movement, memory, learning, and all sensory input. Glial cells—special kinds of cells that serve to nourish and cleanse neurons—were found in significantly greater numbers. And an enzyme called acetylcholinesterase that allows for faster and more efficient transmission of impulses among brain cells was found to be more active. In short, brain development was heavily influenced by experience. Thus, it seems very plausible to suggest that in humans neonatal experiences (and perhaps prenatal experiences as well) could have a very significant impact on brain growth and hence the development of intelligence.

Now let's consider the five arguments that Herrnstein and Murray advance for their genetic explanation. Their first claim is that it seems implausible that environments of blacks and whites could be sufficiently different to account for the differences in IQ scores. But if our alternate explanation is correct, the entire environment need not be greatly different to account for the differences in IQ scores. Only one dimension needs to differ—neonatal and prenatal stimulation in the particular type of intellectual activity that IQ tests measure. Their second claim, the plausibility argument based on the existence of profile differences, is similarly not compelling. This also can be easily understood as cultural differences in stimulation at the prenatal or neonatal stage. In fact, as we can see from the study by Rosenzweig et al. (1972), prenatal and neonatal stimulation can potentially account for Herrnstein and Murray's third claim as well—the physiological difference in neurological reaction time.

Their fourth claim, the one concerning differences in adoptive children, seems at first to be compelling, but it is important to note that no data were included on age at adoption and no controls were even attempted for differences in neonatal and prenatal experiences. Thus, this claim is not persuasive.

And the fifth claim, that genetics is a compelling mechanism because of low African IQ scores, is weak on many grounds. Perhaps the most telling is that IQ scores of American immigrant groups have risen very substantially within a few decades of immigration. For example,[22]

The results of World War I mental tests conducted among American soldiers born in Russia—the great majority of whom were Jews—showed such low scores as to cause Carl Brigham, creator of the Scholastic Aptitude Test, to declare that these results "disprove the popular belief that the Jew is highly intelligent." Within a decade, however, Jews in the United States were scoring above the national average on mental tests, and the data in *The Bell Curve* indicate that they are far above the national average in IQ. (p. 34)

Thus, it is not surprising that Africans, who have not experienced the factors in American language or culture that account for these dramatic increases in scores, would score lower.

In short, then, we find that Herrnstein and Murray's argument that genetics is a causal factor in explaining observed IQ differences is not compelling. Furthermore, contextual norms are significant here. Scientific studies normally try to maintain a high standard for the plausibility of causal claims. But on an issue as controversial and potentially divisive as this one, an even higher standard is needed. Herrnstein and Murray[23] assert, "*We cannot think of a legitimate argument why any encounter between individual whites and blacks need be affected by the knowledge that an aggregate difference in measured intelligence is genetic rather than environmental.*" But they are missing the effect that their claim has on African Americans—Herrnstein and Murray's claim is heard as an assertion that African Americans as a group are genetically inferior. Compassion alone should dictate that their claim ought not be publicly made without overwhelmingly compelling evidence and the authors do not have such evidence.

▓ NOTES

1. See Davis (1985).
2. Mill, as quoted by Turner (1986).
3. Mill, as quoted in Turner (1986).
4. Pearson as quoted in Turner (1986, p. 225).
5. For an extended treatment of this notion, see Suppes (1970).
6. One classic exception is the field trial of the Salk polio vaccine in which a double-blind experiment (neither the children receiving the injections nor their doctors knew who received the vaccine and who received the placebo) was conducted that involved millions of children. The result was a convincing demonstration that the vaccine did indeed significantly reduce the likelihood of the disease.
7. A very readable introductory discussion of Lazarsfeld's principles can be found in Babbie (1986, Chap. 3).
8. See Turner (1986, pp. 61-67) for a more extended discussion of this example.

9. Turner (1986, p. 64).

10. This paragraph is based on the article by B. W. Brown, Jr., in Tanur (1972).

11. Suppes (1970).

12. For example, see the works by Glymour, Scheines, Spirtes, and Kelly (1987); and by Spirtes, Glymour, and Scheines (1993).

13. See Davis (1985). The entire booklet is on this topic.

14. Herrnstein and Murray (1994, p. 98).

15. Perhaps one could argue that genetics is such a variable, but again we don't have a clear enough definition of "genetics" as used in this context to measure it in a way that would allow correlation with IQ score. But note that there is no *a priori* reason to say that genetics could never be such a third variable. To accomplish this, we would have to identify which portions of the genetic code are responsible for race, which parts are responsible for intelligence differences, and demonstrate that variations in these two genetic factors are correlated.

16. Herrnstein and Murray (1994).

17. Herrnstein and Murray (1994, pp. 283-284).

18. Herrnstein and Murray (1994).

19. Herrnstein and Murray (1994).

20. Such differences could be of many types. For instance, there could be different cultural patterns for how parents interact with neonatal children. Alternatively, there could be significant dietary differences for pregnant mothers and/or neonatal children.

21. See Rosenzweig, Bennett, and Diamond (1972).

22. See Sowell (1995).

23. Herrnstein and Murray (1994, p. 313).

Models and Policy Making

FORMAL POLICY ANALYSIS AND PUBLIC NORMS

In the last five chapters we have considered each step in what we have called the "information cycle," exploring the norms that ought to inform the process of modeling, measuring, drawing inferences, and explaining cause and effect relationships. To complete our study, we turn to the relationship between modeling with data in the human sciences and policy making—the practical use of information to affect the world around us.

"Policy making" does not refer only to the public policy of Washington, D.C. or other political centers. In principle, policy making is simply the last part of the information cycle, the step that brings all of the earlier stages to bear in affecting the real world. Thus, human resource managers who use testing to make hiring decisions are engaged in policy making—applying models, human measurements, and inferences about job applicants to decisions that shape an actual firm's future. Housing officials who use models to study occupancy rates or racial migration patterns also are engaged in policy making; so are social workers who use models to

179

compare the likely effects of different interventions, mall managers who gather data to identify problems in the allocation of retailing space, journalists who interpret public opinion polls or economic indicators, third world development agencies that use mathematical methods to evaluate development projects, and school boards that use formal measurements to reward teachers or counteract discrimination. These are examples of the policy-making phase of the information cycle. Though one might distinguish between "policy analysis" (the study of various policy options) and "policy making" (the act of choosing and implementing a policy option), we will use the phrases interchangeably to refer to the entire "study-choose-implement" process at the end of the information cycle.

Though policy making is a very broad category (in fact, partly *because* it is so broad), we can learn much about it by focusing our study on some facets of the policy-making process in political centers like Washington, D.C. As we shall see, this political policy making forms an archetype for other policy making, and the rise in the use of data and models for political policy making has encouraged and even required similar usage elsewhere.

Our aim throughout the book has been to consider the capabilities and limitations of formal modeling in the social sciences, in hopes of clarifying the norms that should govern modeling and the use of data. We bring closure to this discussion, and point back to it, by showing in this chapter how the kinds of norms we have been advocating could be helpful in policy making. We will first briefly review some recent experience with the use of social sciences in policy making. Among other things, this discussion helps to explain why the habits of positivism have persisted in the social sciences after positivism had been discredited by philosophers of science. Then we consider some lessons to be learned. We argue from experience that the policy-making process seems by nature to require a normed approach. This leads to a review of the norms we have proposed throughout the book.

▓ THE CAMELOT ATTITUDE

Although one can find examples of the use of data and models in public policy making throughout modern history, policy analysis that drew on the work of the human sciences entered the U.S. public spotlight in the 1960s under the influence of the Kennedy administration. The administrative changes introduced by Defense Secretary McNamara culminated in the use of planning, programming, and budgeting systems throughout the federal administration and its programs. Large empirical and survey studies accompanied this expansion of scientific policy analysis, covering the spectrum of topics from administrative reforms to birth control attitude-and-behavior surveys, from school bussing and "white flight" to the proposal and evaluation of Medicare.

This ascendancy of formal policy analysis was accompanied by certain predispositions about the nature of policy making, the objectivity of the social sciences, and the role of the professional policy advisor. President Kennedy[1] phrased a common attitude of the day at the White House Economic Conference in 1962.

> The fact of the matter is that most of the problems, or at least many of them that we now face, are technical problems, are administrative problems. They are very sophisticated judgments which do not lend themselves to the great sort of "passionate movements" which have stirred this country so often in the past. Now they deal with questions which are beyond the comprehension of most men. (p. xvi)

A belief that the country had finally reached a broad consensus on the relevant norms (such as promoting a free economic order while actively promoting access to this order among the marginalized) was taken to imply that there remained fewer controversies than managerial obstacles with technical solutions. Social surveys, careful professional planning, and evaluation research were held out as important, generally value-neutral sources for the improvement of society. The main norms involved for the analyst were to be common standards of professional accuracy in reporting data.

This approach to policy analysis left the advisor with a moral burden in affecting the distribution of power, income, and participation. Yet it simultaneously viewed the advisor as a morally detached, passive analyst. These tendencies were amplified by several features of the contemporary political world.

■ Formal policy analysis was being applied to programs that were expanding rapidly in scope and funding. The funding for analysis and evaluation was also expanding rapidly. Analysts were charged with quickly making new agencies and programs work as they were intentioned, on a relatively brief time budget.[2]

■ Program funding usually was provided, subject to evaluations and other administrative regulations. This pushed the social and human sciences beyond descriptive surveys into the analysis of causes of problems and effectiveness of interventions. As we have seen, this study of causality was generally done without a consideration of the normative framework upon which such interpretive work is constructed.[3]

■ Federal funding shifted from university-conducted research toward narrower, policy-directed contracts with research firms (such as Abt Associates, The Rand Corporation, or American Institutes of Research).[4]

■ The appeal of trying to legitimize decisions and even particular decision-makers by citing scientific knowledge grew irresistible,[5] encouraging a positivistic view of social analysts.

■ Policy making became a legitimate graduate degree, a separate and largely technical field. A professional's credibility and advancement hung largely on the ability to maintain the appearance that fact and value are disjoint realms.[6]

Thus, a particular attitude toward social science, analysts, positivism, and the political process became institutionalized through a web of research procedures, administrative and legislative requirements, funding procedures, graduate curricula, and professional reward systems.[7]

▓ THE CAMELOT PROBLEM

Political changes are rarely untainted marvels, rarely absolute failures. Much good came of the changes in policy making that began in the 1960s. Yet there are problems with what we have called "the Camelot attitude."

It might be enough to point out that President Kennedy's address, affirming that most of our remaining problems were ill-suited to "passionate movements" and were beyond comprehension outside the Ivy League, was delivered on the brink of an era best remembered for the Vietnam war and the Civil Rights movement. These hardly illustrate dispassionate technical problems that were beyond the average person's understanding.

Although Camelot may have expected an era of value-free policy analysis, the social-research-based era it ushered in is in fact marked by contention.[8]

> In virtually every major sphere of public policy in which social research has entered, there has been intense debate about the work. The most publicized cases involve public education—as with achievement testing, the Coleman report, school desegregation, and the Head Start Program. But bitter exchanges have occurred in other realms, too. . . . Although "politics" is the usual charge, at root these controversies typically focus on the posture that social scientists *should* take in the policy arena—an ethical question. (p. 340)

We have said that the rise of formal policy analysis was accompanied by certain attitudes about the nature of policy making, the objectivity of the social sciences, and the role of the professional policy advisor. Why was this Camelot conception of social science, analysts, positivism, and the political order likely to be found wanting? At the most general level, this attitude understates a central tension within social science that policy analysis actually forces into prominence: the relationship between modeling and questions of value, meaning, and purpose.[9]

> The task of policy analysis is to bring evidence and interpretation to bear on decision making and social practice. This task involves not only the presentation of evidence about the consequences of pursuing alternate actions but also an interpretation of what it is we are doing in society, why we are doing what we do, and what we might do differently given our puzzlement and worry about what we do. (p. 83)

Policy analysis, perhaps more than anywhere else in the information cycle, is a place where "is" and "ought" are brought together, sometimes in stark contrast.

But this general observation should be fleshed out by considering some details about political policy making. We will consider four main areas. They are not unique to political policy analysis, but their effects elsewhere in social science are somewhat restrained by multiple, diverse analyses of any one situation. These expose the biases and limitations of individual methods and approaches. Policy analysis, on the other hand, is more centralized in funding, more restricted in time frame, and more limited in the number of investigators and peer reviewers.[10]

The Complex Role
of Data and Modeling

We can begin by noting that the role of social science modeling and data in policy making is more complex than mere service as a technical companion to inform the details of difficult tasks.[11]

> In the last few years, studies of the consequences of social science research have led to a reconceptualization of the role of research in the policy process. These studies tend to affirm that immediate and direct linkages between study results and policy decisions are relatively rare. But research does seem to contribute a series of concepts, generalizations, and ideas that often come to permeate policy discussion. . . . Not single findings, one by one, but ideas from social science research appear to affect the development of the policy agenda. Social science research is one of the sources from which participants in the policy process derive their sense of how the world works. (p. 219)

Thus, the effect of social science is more dramatic in forming categories of thought than in the details of any particular piece of work. Though formal analysis sometimes contributes data that are important to a particular issue, its more profound effect comes by altering the explanatory framework within which a problem is considered, the variables that are considered relevant, and the issues that attract attention.[12] General social science *concepts,* such as "externalities,"[13] "community norms," and "social support networks," affect public policy, partly because they help policy makers organize the deluge of information and experience of which they must make sense.[14]

So, the specific pieces of policy analysis are only small bits of information in the ears of policy makers, competing in a symphony of many influences. To make matters even more complicated, many of these influences, including the technical analysis, may be received indirectly.[15]

> Possibly the most significant point to underscore here is that research only occasionally reaches policy actors directly in the form of written reports or even executive summaries of reports. More frequent is the diffusion of research generalizations and ideas through other existing channels—the media, conferences and meetings, expert consultation, conversations with colleagues, and so on. (p. 228)

To the extent that social science policy research is filtered through media sources who are not professional practitioners or who report policy research as "human interest" stories, the most important policy issues in the formal research may be lost in translation.[16]

Thus, the technical details of policy analysis often carry less weight than the general categories in which the analysis is conducted,[17] and even these general categories are often received secondhand by policy makers. This reality underscores the importance of evaluating the frames of reference of the human sciences, the norms, values, and purposes that ultimately drive the technical work but are undervalued by the Camelot attitude. Ellul's concern[18] that technique may displace broader, more significant topics seems especially important in the institutions of policy making.

The Nature of Social Science Findings

A second issue is related to the general problem with positivism: The kind of knowledge the social sciences can deliver is not usually of the technically objective sort that is set apart from considerations of purpose and value. As we saw in Chapters 2 and 4, data themselves do not exhaust meaning but require an interpretation.[19]

> The questions we ask of reality depend upon the perspective we take in approaching the phenomenon, and it is this perspective that shapes the categories we use to impose order and give meaning to reality. In this sense, then, we construe reality by the categories of understanding we impose, the questions we ask, and the perspectives and purposes with which we approach our inquiry. Nevertheless this does not mean that we reject the facticity of the world and its underlying reality. . . . [Yet] we know that nothing we say about reality is definitive, authoritative, and fully settled. There are very few interpretations of reality which are not contentious and could not be questioned by someone who had a different line of thought (theory), or was trying to get somewhere else (purposes), or made use of a different method of understanding, which proceeded by different starting assumptions about what is important to understand in the world (*a priori* assumptions and analytic methods).
>
> In the field of policy, the questions of purpose and values are central. They call attention not only to the factual questions of where I am at the moment but also to where I want to go. Hence, questions of purpose are central in any policy undertaking.[20]

This reality appears to have begun sinking in on policy makers in the early 1970s.[21] Skepticism emerged about the authoritativeness of human science policy studies when concepts like community action, client participation, deinstitutionalization, and the Phillips curve[22] proved less than omnipotent in framing policy issues. Regarding the evaluation methods of the human sciences, policy makers

> gradually became aware that evaluation was not the antiseptic purveyor of universally accepted, objective data. Evaluation research, as all social science research, was suffused with values. As social scientists had long recognized, every stage of the research process—from the formulation of the initial question to the development of conclusions—was punctuated with choices, which were resolved by applying value judgments.[23]

Some research methods do not allow consideration of all of the data relevant to the policy issue at hand or require data that are unreliable. For instance, parts of family-directed social policy were informed by KAP (knowledge-attitude-practice) birth control studies. It was later found that the questionnaires were not understood by a significant number of respondents and that some questions were biased toward particular results.[24] And "striking examples abound of how the selection of outcome measures can determine policy conclusions,"[25] such as judging program success by changes in attitudes of clients (rather than changes in more stubborn behavior) or by counting services rendered (rather than assessing the actual effects of these services).

Thus, social science work is framed by value judgments and subject to serious measurement problems. We have argued[26] that this reality requires normative principles to guide the research effort.

Research Changes Those Observed and Those Observing

Guillemin and Horowitz have described how the policy-oriented, social-scientific study of marginal groups can inadvertently undermine the value of social-scientific study.[27] The authors[28] documented the development of ethnographic studies that culminated, by the late 1960s, in empirical work that opened doors to political action in the name of the group which was described in ways that earlier, qualitative research had failed to achieve. Crossing the threshold from academic work to practical involvement in the mobilization of deviant and marginal groups proved a direct though not irreversible change of role from scientific observer to social actor. (p. 190)

Whereas direct activism by a researcher potentially may undermine the academic quality of the work, one might hope that this could be sniffed out by replication studies with access to the same population. But this is where the problem arises. By studying and "organizing" subpopulations as self-aware groups, the researchers created an opportunity for groups to limit the access of researchers who were not predisposed toward desirable findings.[29]

> The most surprising phenomenon of the times was the rapidity with which the revelatory characteristics of social research and analysis . . . would fail as negotiable policy currency. . . . Once marginal groups could generate their own framework for organization on which to base entitlement, they could make a strong bid for government recognition, representation, and support quite without sociological advocates. . . . Social science was thereby reduced from advocacy to testimony or sometimes testimony as advocacy. . . . The central point of tension became competition with other groups of similar outlook wishing to allocate resources, a competition that disallowed impartial, potentially critical long-term research by social scientists and lent to marginal groups the same defensive restrictions . . . associated with bureaucratic organizations. (pp. 198-199)

In the end, access to the studied group may be granted only on the terms of the group, with predictable effects on the quality of the research.[30]

> The political activation of . . . [studied groups] . . . has profoundly transformed their image. . . . They are now seen as robust interest groups, competing on an equal footing with other groups. . . . [This] signifies a deep change in the research posture that social scientists can take toward these presumably marginal groups. . . . As the price of entrance into future research projects, social scientists are being asked to become increasingly partisan. (p. 204)

The same might be said of other bureaucratic institutions that can impose conditions on access, such as hospitals, prisons, mental institutions, schools, or defense institutions. Organizations that face regulatory review are likely to limit the access of investigators whose review might prove damaging to the institution's survival.

This process is amplified by the funding institutions through which social research is conducted.[31]

> The command that government agency and department heads exert over research has permitted contract houses to do the bulk of policy work, if only because the intellectual fit is far better between the federal bureaucracy and Abt, Rand, Bendix, or Systems Development Corporation than between the same bureaucracy and a university environment. . . . The net effect of the increasing bureaucratization of channels of funding and program evaluation has been even sharper competition among organizations and communities acting as special interests totally resistant to nonpartisan inquiry which exposes them to closer observation. (p. 202)

The result of this process not only has been a loss of objectivity and reliability but deformed development of the policy analysis profession as a whole.[32]

> Short of a total retreat from empirical research, social ethnographers have had little choice but to let the definition of the fieldwork contract rest exclusively with informants as they saw the potential use of social science. . . . The intellectual and professional price for continued ethnographic access has been high. Major comparative work which would relieve community and small-group studies of their unstinting resistance to generalization has not been forthcoming, nor has the successful integration of qualitative and quantitative methods or an historical appreciation of national development emerged from the many efforts in applied research. (p. 200)

Thus, the Camelot attitude inadvertently set in motion a process with the potential to seriously debase the policy analysis it valued.

Further Effects of The Funding Apparatus

We have suggested that the funding process for formal policy analysis does not leave it entirely uncorrupted. Sponsors have limits and interests, and analysts compete for their money. Thus, researchers cannot be considered an entirely disinterested band. How to frame questions, whom to interview, which success indicators are appropriate, how to weigh various influences, which conclusions to highlight, which kinds of work are recognized as helpful—these often are influenced, if not dictated, by the funding apparatus.[33] Research is likely to be limited to the variables the funding agency has authority to manipulate, and policy options are constrained by the current agency guidelines. Even the entire conceptual basis may be determined by the sponsor.[34] As an early example that is still having repercussions, consider the long-term damage done to individuals, military leadership, society, and the human sciences when the Army chose to rely on mass administration of an IQ instrument, the Alpha test, to identify "leadership material" during World War I.

By now, we are far afield from the vision of policy analysis as a value-free arbitration of technical issues. The nature of policy making, the objectivity of the social sciences, and the role of the professional analyst each has been misunderstood, with repercussions that have inadvertently cheapened social research. We should be viewing policy analysis differently.

DATA, MODELING, AND NORMS: FIRST STEPS

The myth of Camelot always has held a fascination. The image of strong, young, idealistic people changing the existing order and establishing justice is enormously winsome. But the round table of Arthur's time faltered because its king and knights paid insufficient attention to their own fallibility and limits.

This is not a bad metaphor for the role of social science in policy making. The fallibilities of human science that were underrated in the 1960s arose from the limits of the methods themselves and the need to accompany them with contextual norms. But it would not be right to reject the use of social science data and models simply because they have been used without full recognition of their limits. The alternatives all have problems of their own. Instead, policy making needs to recognize the limits of data and models and use them as fully as possible within these limits.

The attitude that policy analysis is primarily a technical exercise, within which the discussion of norms is awkward or inappropriate, led to weak policy analysis. In this book we have tried to sketch an alternative, in which the consideration of norms and purpose would be a routine part of the use of data and models. Beyond making a case for *what* should be done, we hope that this book has begun to explore *how* it can be done. Our analysis of policy making highlights the importance of the normative principles we have developed throughout our discussion of the information cycle. Thus, we close with a digest that draws together this book's analysis of the norms that should inform the use of data and models in the social and human sciences.

■ Those who are not professional modelers should remain aware that alternate models for a situation will lead to different "scientific" results and policy; various models usually expose only some facets of a situation and even then only apply under the specific conditions assumed in the model.[35]

■ Users therefore need to remain open to several different ways to model and explore a situation, rather than becoming locked-in to a specific approach; they should especially beware of applying a model of routine activity to exceptional circumstances, of "typing" persons through modeling, and of using abstracted models of causality to reconstruct the motives or decision-making processes of individuals.

■ Analysts should use the most powerful research design available, with a wide, appropriate range of outcome measures,[36] permitting a range of alternative explanations and results to be explored. The motivations and limits of each choice should be discussed. Choices of topic or method influenced by the source of funding should be made especially clear. This becomes especially important because, to the extent that modeling is powerful and useful, there is some danger that groups who cannot afford good modelers will find themselves at an increasing disadvantage.

■ Analysts must carefully represent the completeness and relevance of their work, along with the limitations of the data and predictions. Social phenomena are so complex we always (at least partially) misrepresent them; situations are often dynamic, some influential variables may be absent, and other variables may be measured through proxies chosen primarily because they could be measured. Thus, empirical methods face limits, and a large dose of humility is required when studying social phenomena.

■ When controls on variables are impossible, we are dependent on careful randomization. When randomization is not done, the resulting information ought not be very persuasive. The best subject matter for empirical work is routine, repeatable situations.[37] The potential for a study to change those being studied, in a way that will inhibit the access of future researchers, should be considered when designing a research project.

■ The questions analysts ask and the data they gather are strongly influenced by the methods they choose to employ. Social scientists, because they are dealing with people, always must be acutely conscious of the methods they are using and of how these methods can direct their thinking. They must be willing to step outside their usual collection of methods to explore possibilities that would otherwise be unthinkable.

■ Although objectivity may never be strictly expected—we may never completely transcend the personal characteristics we bring to an investigation, and information must be interpreted in light of the context in which it was generated—objectivity can be approximated and serves as a regulative ideal. For example, the context within which the research originated can be made clear.

■ Modelers need to deliberately create openness for the evaluation of models[38] and the assumptions, limits, and values implicit in them. Modelers should discuss which aspects of the model are transferable to reality, what features of reality are better studied by a different model, and which qualitative variables are absent from the model. Data and methodology should be fully accessible so that replication and respecification can happen.

■ Every study should explore and report the robustness of its model. Cumulative replication and respecification are harder in the social sciences than in the natural sciences; testing the fragility of assumptions should not be left to unconnected later articles.

■ Professional work must be laid bare for peer review,[39] replication, and analysis of the same data from different methodological and conceptual frameworks. Social science is not as cumulative as natural science, but it would be much more cumulative if data were freely available for use and inspection by others, especially others with different policy predispositions. Policy research seems to be in special need of this advice, where disinterested peer review is not always typical. "Much of the debate in these policy research controversies has involved empirical claims that could have been at least partially settled by equal access to the same data sets."[40]

■ Modelers' education needs to be broad and liberal so that they can examine the modeled situation from several points of view.

■ The many benefits of measurement—power to predict, transcend individual subjectivity, resolve error, enhance social justice, make fine distinctions, and accumulate knowledge—create strong temptations to cut corners by trying to quantify without an adequate basis.

■ Therefore, modelers should carefully determine what is important enough to measure before trying to measure it. They should then decide which measurement scale[41] is reasonable for the characteristic in question, especially avoiding the temptation to treat attributes as if they behave like numbers if no justification has been given. Modelers then must live within the bounds imposed by the characteristics of the appropriate measurement scale.

■ Modelers should listen carefully to critics of the particular proxy variables chosen in a study. For example, IQ scores illustrate a common problem—the scores can be useful, but to call them "intelligence" is (at best) presumptuous. It is altogether too easy to forget that a proxy is merely a proxy for the actual attribute under study. Modelers should be especially skeptical of the results of "What if" questionnaire items, because the answers are often distant proxies for the actual behavior that would be observed.

■ The potential effect of human measurement on those being studied also should be considered as an ethical constraint on human measurement; measurement of people should only be done when sufficient preparation has been made to deal with the consequences.

■ Random error terms (the differences between a model's forecasts and our actual observations) convey information about the abstractions, approximations, ignorance, and measurement problems involved in a model. The drawing of inferences therefore should involve a careful inspection of the residuals between the data and the model's predictions.

■ The formal "level of significance" of a result always must be held in the context of the overall reasonableness of the entire model: its abstractions, specification of the situation, measurement scales for the variables, quality of data, and attendance to residual errors. The empirical analyst must regard inferences as contributory evidence, not as proof that removes the need for insight, common sense, and persuasion.

■ We should be especially skeptical of stated levels of statistical significance when the (a) social processes under study are extremely complex, with many auxiliary hypotheses complicating the primary hypotheses; (b) entity being measured is not clearly definable, or there is a poorly developed theory of the entity and its relationship to the measurable variables, or when the measurement instrument is not precise and reliable; (c) functional forms and/or statistical methods employed are not consistent with the measurement scale; and (d) specifications of the model and its functional forms are not clearly justified by reference to the actual situation being modeled.

■ Social and decision sciences often must live with soft data and few controlled experiments; it may be difficult to draw hard inferences. A demonstration of causation involves even higher standards, as we reviewed in Chapter 8. Correlation does not establish causation, and probabilistically causal arguments cannot be applied to individuals. Special reflection is due when a causal hypothesis would be harmful to some people if incorrect but helpful to others if correct.

■ Analysts must be self-aware about the value commitments that drive the many small but cumulative choices that are the fabric of policy analysis. The conceptual "spin" that this introduces to the work should be made clear to others.

▓ NOTES

1. Callahan and Jennings (1983).
2. See, for example, Warwick and Pettigrew (1983, p. 343).
3. See, for example, Weiss (1983, p. 215).
4. Warwick and Pettigrew (1983, pp. 337-338).
5. See, for example, Bellah (1983, p. 51).
6. Rein (1983, p. 85).
7. Jennings (1983, p. 7).
8. Warwick and Pettigrew (1983).
9. Rein (1983).
10. Warwick and Pettigrew (1983, pp. 344-345).
11. Weiss (1983). See also Warwick and Pettigrew (1983) for a bibliography of the relevant literature.
12. Weiss (1983, p. 226).
13. Externalities are benefits or costs of an action that are not borne by the parties engaged in the action. Smokestack pollution is a classic example. Some of the costs of producing the product are "exported" to people living miles from the production site and therefore not borne by the people who buy and sell the factory's goods. The result: The product is artificially cheap, and therefore too much of it is produced and purchased.
14. See Weiss (1983, p. 230).
15. See Weiss (1983).
16. See, for example, Warwick and Pettigrew (1983, p. 359).
17. Lindblom and Cohen (1979) use this as a basis to argue that social research findings *ought not* have much effect on public policy, favoring interactive problem solving and causal analysis.

18. We discussed Ellul's critique in Chapter 1.

19. For instance, information from the 1920s and 1930s that is used to interpret the great depression as an instance of too little government intervention also can be used to argue that the depression was caused and extended by government interventions of the wrong kind. See, for example, Carson (1991, pp. 35ff).

20. Rein (1983, pp. 94-95).

21. For a review of the process, see Weiss (1983, pp. 216ff).

22. The Phillips curve presented a historical (negative) correlation between the rate of inflation and the rate of unemployment. It was thought (by policy makers) to imply that a lower unemployment rate could be "bought" at the expense of a higher inflation rate. The late 1960s demonstrated that the negative correlation was a special case; if unemployment rates were pushed low for any length of time, or if oil prices jumped significantly, the relationship between inflation and unemployment shifted. Temporary reductions in unemployment had only bought permanently higher inflation rates, with little long-run change in unemployment rates.

23. Weiss (1983, p. 217). Robert Bellah (1983) makes similar observations.

Practical social scientists do not claim the degree of scientific precision to which technological social science aspires, partly because they do not think it is possible in the study of human affairs. . . . They are not technical specialists looking across a great gulf at other technical specialists calling themselves philosophers. Similarly, they are not purveyors of neutral information, the policy implications of which are of no concern to them. Ethical and policy concerns have determined their research interests from the beginning and they are acutely aware that the way data are presented always has policy implications. (p. 63)

Likewise another commentator (Sjoberg, 1975) says,

The more one delves into the massive literature on evaluation research, the more cognizant one becomes of the deep-seated ethical and political implications of the social scientist's efforts, whether direct or indirect, to evaluate the performance of individuals or the programs of ongoing organizations. The political and ethical dilemmas are especially troublesome in the evaluation of experimental programs. (p. 29)

24. Warwick and Pettigrew (1983, p. 343) discussed the use of (a) KAP (knowledge-attitude-practice) birth control surveys; (b) race-and-IQ studies that require an unjustifiable distinction between hereditary and environmental factors; (c) the tendency to fund large-sample cross-sectional surveys to evaluate effectiveness of diverse federal programs, whether the research design is appropriate to the program or not. Page 353 pursues the weaknesses in the KAP surveys at more length.

25. Warwick and Pettigrew (1983, p. 349).

26. See Chapters 4 through 6.

27. See Guillemin and Horowitz (1983).

28. Guillemin and Horowitz (1983, p. 190).

29. Guillemin and Horowitz (1983).

30. Guillemin and Horowitz (1983).

31. Guillemin and Horowitz (1983).

32. Guillemin and Horowitz (1983).

33. See, for example, Hanft (1983, p. 242), Warwick and Pettigrew (1983, p. 342).

34. See Warwick and Pettigrew (1983, p. 342) for several examples. See Warwick and Pettigrew (1983, p. 349) for a discussion of this phenomenon in evaluating energy conservation programs and family planning initiatives. See Rein (1983, p. 93) for comment about Swedish policy analysis that chooses success indicators that favor Swedish social policy.

35. "Multiple rather than single research methods should be employed in complex areas of policy or when public debate about the research findings is likely to occur. If the resources are not available for multiple research methods, such critical work should not be attempted" (Warwick & Pettigrew, 1983, p. 362).

36. Warwick and Pettigrew (1983, pp. 350, 363).

37. Studies that aim to identify a problem or evaluate an intervention might draw less crucially on disputed theories of cause and effect than studies comparing interventions. See Murray (1983, pp. 314-318).

38. See, for example, Wallace (1994).

39. See, for example, Murray (1983, p. 330).

40. Warwick and Pettigrew (1983, p. 358).

41. See Chapters 5 and 6 for a fuller development of the notion of measurement scales and the attributes and limits of the five options.

Glossary

Antirealism The view that things external to the person are granted their structure by the thought processes of humans; contrasted to the verifiability principle of meaning of logical positivists.

Conditional probability The probability that an event B will occur, when it is known that some event A has occurred, is the conditional probability of B given A.

Confidence interval A range of numbers that, with some degree of certainty, is claimed by a statistical test to include the true value of an item in the real world.

Contextual norms See extrinsic norms.

Correlation Two variables are correlated if the value that one variable takes on systematically changes as the level of the other variable changes.

Definitions

Lexical A dictionary definition; a list of popular uses of a word.

Essential A definition that captures the essence of an idea.

Operational A definition that specifies a procedure by which one can determine whether an object or event is an instance of the concept being defined.

196

Disciplinary matrix In Kuhn's work, the shared items that allow professionals to communicate clearly and reach a consensus; they include shared symbols, values, and beliefs. These are usually communicated through exemplars.

Duhem's irrefutability thesis (or the Duhem-Quine thesis) Tests of any primary hypothesis involve so many auxiliary assumptions that the original, primary hypothesis is insulated from a hard rejection; there are no definitive counter-facts to a primary hypothesis.

Equivalence class A collection of items that all can be regarded as mutually equivalent, at least as far as the characteristic of interest is concerned. An equivalence relation must satisfy three mathematical properties—it must be symmetric, reflexive, and transitive.

Exemplar In Kuhn's work, the examples of professional work that are accepted by the scientific community as models for how a particular subject should be approached.

Extrinsic ("contextual") norms Principles of right action that are typically regarded as common-sense or prima facie duties, not arising from the capabilities or limitations of any particular methodology or from the internal norms of scientific and mathematical work such as truthfulness, simplicity, and so forth; norms that govern what *should* be done, apart from questions of what *can* be done.

Information cycle The process of generating human information, from framing questions and models through measurement, hypothesizing, inference, establishing causality, and forming policy or making decisions.

Information Data and any summaries or inferences derived from data.

Intersubjective agreement Agreement between two persons on an issue. For example, two might disagree about whether a backpack is heavy, but weighing the backpack may lead to agreement that it weighs thirty pounds. Measurement has led to intersubjective agreement.

Intrinsic ("methodological") norms Norms that arise from the capabilities and limitations of the processes of collecting data and developing models and from the internal norms of scientific and mathematical work such as truthfulness, simplicity, and so forth; contrasted with extrinsic/contextual norms.

Linear programming A mathematical model for normative decision making, in which objectives and constraints are represented by equations and inequalities; the objective is then maximized, subject to the constraints.

Loss function A function that indicates how much is lost by a statistical faulty estimate of some real-world item.

Measurement Scales

Nominal Categories, which might not even involve numbers (uniform numbers, telephone numbers)

Ordinal Rankings (best to worst, first to last; student grades, baseball team rankings).

Interval Measurement scales on which addition and subtraction are meaningful, but not multiplication or division (fahrenheit temperature, calendar time).

Ratio Measurement scales on which addition, subtraction, multiplication and division are all meaningful (mass, length, time).

Absolute Allows no changes in scale, as it is not measured relative to a unit (counting, probability).

Methodological norms See intrinsic norms.

Misspecification error An error made when drawing inferences about the world, caused by excluding relevant issues from consideration or including irrelevant issues.

Model A framework of analysis that abstracts from the details of the real world, in an attempt to highlight the explanation of phenomena or obtain forecasts.

Naturalism An attempt to explain phenomena within the physical universe by reference only to the natural realm; denies supernatural or metaphysical entities.

Normative decision making Prescriptive modeling of decisions, in order to identify the "best" decision in a particular situation; contrasted to descriptive models that describe the process through which a decision is made.

Null hypothesis In statistics, typically an assumption that there is no significant difference between treatments. The null hypothesis is assumed unless substantive evidence can be found to reject it.

Policy making The final step in the information cycle; the choice and implementation of an act that brings the earlier stages of the information cycle to bear in affecting the real world.

Positivism A school of thought based on the idea that there can be no knowledge except that which rests on sensory observations; these observations are taken to be the objective material from which theories and beliefs are formed.

Power The probability of appropriately rejecting a null hypothesis that is false.

Pretest bias A statistical test's stated level of significance may be misleading, because the test is built on the results of other tests that are assumed to be correct. These other tests are incorrect with some positive probability. Therefore the stated level of significance for the final test is an exaggeration. It is said that this final test suffers from a pretest bias.

Proxy A variable that serves as a measurable substitute for a different variable under study that is, for some reason, not measurable.

Random error term A term or variable used in statistical studies to represent the influence of errors in measurements or unspecified excluded variables. Random error terms measure the distance between what was observed and what was expected from the model.

Randomization Selection or assignment procedures that guarantee that each subject is equally likely to be selected or be assigned in some particular way.

Replication studies Scholarship that seeks to reproduce and confirm earlier work.

Representation theorem As used most often in this book, a mathematical proof, that a given set of axioms is sufficient to establish a meaningful correspondence between a characteristic under study and the real numbers. This is used to establish that a particular measurement scale is appropriate to the situation under study. More generally, representation theorems are used to establish correspondences with other sets than just the real numbers.

Robust A model is robust when its conclusions do not change abruptly due to small changes in assumptions, observations, or variables.

Significance, level or degree of The probability of committing a Type I error in a statistical test.

Spurious correlation A correlation that is measured between two variables, when there is no cause and effect relationship between the variables.

Structural analysis The use of mathematics to experiment with ideas, in hopes of exploring what might be possible rather than exploring what actually exists. Banzhaf's power index and Arrow's impossibility theorem are examples of structural analysis.

Technique When used by Ellul, Barrett, and others, technique refers to a method of thinking that seeks to reduce activities to routines (or "algorithms") that can then be optimized.

Test of significance A statistical test that quantifies the likelihood that a variable or variables under study exhibit a specified amount of difference from one another or from a particular value.

Type I error The mistake of rejecting a true null hypothesis.

Type II error The mistake of retaining a false null hypothesis.

Type III error The use of a good model for the wrong situation.

Verifiability principle of meaning The logical positivist's assertion that statements that can not be verified by direct sensory experience are meaningless.

References

Allport, G. W. (1958). *The nature of prejudice.* Garden City, NY: Doubleday.

Anderson, D. R., Sweeney, D. J., & Williams, T. A. (1993). *Statistics for business and economics* (5th ed.). Minneapolis: West.

Arney, W. R. (1990). *Understanding statistics in the social sciences.* New York: Freeman.

Arrow, K. J. (1960). Decision theory and the choice of a level of significance for the t-test. In I. Olkin, S. G. Ghurye, W. Hoeffding, W. G. Mdow, & H. B. Mann (Eds.), *Contributions to probability and statistics: Essays in honor of Harold Hotelling.* Stanford: Stanford University Press.

Arrow, K. J., & Raynaud, H. (1986). *Social choice and multicriterion decision making.* Cambridge: MIT Press.

Babbie, E. (1986). *The practice of social research* (4th ed.) Belmont, CA: Wadsworth.

Banzhaf, J., III. (1965). Weighted voting doesn't work. *Rutgers Law Review, 19,* 317-343.

Barrett, W. (1978). *The illusion of technique: A search for meaning in a technological civilization.* New York: Anchor/Doubleday.

Bellah, R. N. (1983). Social science as practical reason. In D. Callahan & B. Jennings (Eds.), *Ethics, the social sciences, and policy analysis.* New York: Plenum.

Bergstrom, T. C. (1995). On the evolution of altruistic ethical rules for siblings. *American Economic Review, 85*(1), 58-81.

Brams, S. J., Lucas, W. F., & Straffin, P. D., Jr. (Eds.). (1983). *Political and related models, modules in applied mathematics* (Vol. 2). New York/Berlin: Springer-Verlag.

Bridgman, P. W. (1927). *The logic of modern physics.* New York: MacMillan.

Brown, B. W., Jr. (1972). Statistics, scientific method, and smoking. In J. Tanur (Ed.), *Statistics: A guide to the unknown.* San Francisco: Holdin-Day.

Burtless, G. (1995). The case for randomized field trials in economic and policy research. *Journal of Economic Perspectives, 9*(2), 63-84.

Butterfield, H. (1957). *The origins of modern science.* London: G. Bell and Sons.

Callahan, D., & Jennings, B. (Eds). (1983). *Ethics, the social sciences, and policy analysis.* New York: Plenum.

Campbell, D., & Stanley, J. (1963). *Experimental and quasi-experimental designs for research.* Chicago: Rand McNally.

Carson, R. B. (1991). *Macroeconomic issues today: Alternative approaches* (5th ed.). New York: St. Martin's.

Comte, A. (1970). *Introduction to positive philosophy* (F. Ferré, Trans.). Indianapolis: Bobbs-Merrill. (Original work published 1868)

Cook, D., & Campbell, D. T. (1979). *Quasi-experimentation: Design and analysis issues for field settings.* Chicago: Rand McNally.

Daellenbach, J. G., George, J. A., & McNickle, D. C. (1983). *Introduction to operations research techniques.* Newton, MA: Allyn and Bacon.

Darnell, A. C., & Evans, J. L. (1990). *The limits of econometrics.* Brookfield, VT: Edward Elgar.

Davis, J. A. (1985). *The logic of causal order* (Sage University Paper series on Quantitative Applications in the Social Sciences, series no. 55). Newbury Park, CA: Sage.

Davis, P. J., & Hersh, R. (1986). *Descartes' dream: The world according to mathematics.* Boston: Houghton Mifflin.

Ellul, J. (1964). *The technological society.* New York: Knopf.

Ellul, J. (1980). *The technological system.* New York: Continuum.

Ellul, J. (1990). *The technological bluff.* Grand Rapids, MI: Wm. B. Eerdmans.

Feige, E. (1975). The consequences of journal editorial policies and a suggestion for revision. *Journal of Political Economy, 83*(4), 1291-1296.

Frankena, W. K. (1973). *Ethics.* Englewood Cliffs, NJ: Prentice Hall.

Glymour, C., Scheines, R., Spirtes, P., & Kelly, K. (1987). *Discovering causal structure: Artificial intelligence, philosophy of science, and statistical modeling.* San Diego: Academic Press.

Gould, S. J. (1981). *The mismeasure of man.* New York: Norton.

Guillemin, J., & Horowitz, I. L. (1983). Social research and political advocacy: New stages and old problems in integrating science and values. In D. Callahan & B. Jennings (Eds.), *Ethics, the social sciences, and policy analysis.* New York: Plenum.

Gusfield, D., & Irving, R. W. (1989). *The stable marriage problem.* Cambridge: MIT Press.

Gwartney, J., & Haworth, C. (1974). Employer costs and discrimination: The case of baseball. *Journal of Political Economy, 82*(4), 873-882.

Hanft, R. S. (1983). Use of social science data for policy analysis and policymaking. In D. Callahan & B. Jennings (Eds.), *Ethics, the social sciences, and policy analysis.* New York: Plenum.

Heckman, J. J., & Smith, J. A. (1995). Assessing the case for social experiments. *Journal of Economic Perspectives, 9*(2), 85-110.

ICPSR. *Guide to resources and services, 1993-1994.* P.O. Box 1248, Ann Arbor, MI.

Herrnstein, R. J., & Murray, C. (1994). *The bell curve.* New York: Free Press.

Hock, R. R. (1992). *Forty studies that changed psychology.* Englewood Cliffs, NJ: Prentice Hall.

Holmes, T. H., & Rahe, R. H. (1967). The social readjustment scale. *Journal of Psychosomatic Research, 11*, 213-218.

Jennings, B. (1983). Interpretive social science and policy analysis. In D. Callahan & B. Jennings (Eds.), *Ethics, the social sciences, and policy analysis.* New York: Plenum.

Kant, I. (1959). *Foundations of the metaphysics of morals, and what is enlightenment?* (L. B. White, Trans.). Indianapolis: Bobbs-Merrill. (Original work published 1785)

Kant, I. (1965). *Critique of pure reason* (N. K. Smith, Trans.). New York: St. Martin's. (Original work published 1781)

Keeney, R. L. (1996). *Value-focused thinking: A path to creative decision making.* Cambridge, MA: Harvard University Press.

Kline, M. (1953). *Mathematics in western culture.* New York: Oxford University Press.

Kling, R., & Iaconno, S. (1988, June). The mobilization of support for computerization: The role of computerization movements. *Social Problems, 35*(3), 226-243.

Kmenta, J. (1971). *Elements of econometrics.* New York: Macmillan.

Koblitz, N. (1981). Mathematics as propaganda. In L. A. Steen (Ed.), *Mathematics tomorrow.* New York/Berlin: Springer-Verlag.

Kramer, J. J., & Conoley, J. C. (Eds.). (1992). *Buros' mental measurement handbook.* Lincoln: University of Nebraska Press.

Krantz, D. H., Luce, R. D., Suppes, P., & Tversky, A. (1971). *Foundations of measurement* (Vol. I). New York: Academic Press.

Kuhn, T. (1962). *The structure of scientific revolutions.* Chicago: University of Chicago Press.

Kyberg, H. (1984). *Theory and measurement.* Cambridge, UK: Cambridge University Press.

LaPiere, R. T. (1934). Attitudes and action. *Social Forces, 13*, 230-237.

Lieberson, S. (1985). *Making it count: The improvement of social research and theory.* Berkeley: University of California Press.

Lindblom, C. E., & Cohen, D. K. (1979). *Usable knowledge.* New Haven, CT: Yale University Press.

Lindert, P. H. (1991). *International economics* (9th ed.). Burr Ridge, IL: Irwin.

Lovell, M. C. (1983, February). Data mining. *Review of Economics and Statistics, 45*, pp. 1-12.

Luce, R. D., Krantz, D. H., Suppes, P., & Tversky, A. (1990). *Foundations of measurements* (Vol. III). New York: Academic Press.

MacIntyre, A. (1981). *After culture.* South Bend, IN: University of Notre Dame Press.

MacIntyre, A. (1988). *Whose justice? Which rationality?* London: Duckworth.

MacKay, A. F. (1980). *Arrow's theorem: The paradox of social choice.* New Haven, CT: Yale University Press.

Maki, D. P., & Thompson, M. (1973). *Mathematical models and applications.* Englewood Cliffs: Prentice Hall.

Marsden, G. (1994). *The soul of the American university: From protestant establishment to established nonbelief.* New York: Oxford University Press.

Masterman, M. (1970). The nature of a paradigm. In I. Lakatos & A. Musgrave (Eds.), *Criticism and the growth of knowledge.* Cambridge, UK: Cambridge University Press.

McCloskey, D. N. (1985, May). The loss function has been mislaid: The rhetoric of significance tests. *American Economic Review, 75*, 201-205.

McCloskey, H.J. (1969). *Meta-ethics and normative ethics.* The Hague, The Netherlands: Martinus Nijhoff.

McNamara, R. (1995). *In retrospect: The tragedy and lessons of Vietnam.* New York: Random House.

Meredith, J. (1995, March). What is empirical research? *Decision Line, 29*(2), p. 10.

Miller, D. (Ed.) (1985). *Popper selections.* Princeton, NJ: Princeton University Press.

Moore, D. S. (1995). *The basic practice of statistics.* New York: Freeman.

Morrison, D.E., & Henkel R.E. (1970). *The significance test controversy.* Hawthorne, NY: Aldine.

Murphy, L. L., Conoley, J. C., & Impara, J. C. (Eds.). (1994). *Tests in print IV.* Lincoln: University of Nebraska Press.

Murray, T. H. (1983). Partial knowledge. In D. Callahan & B. Jennings (Eds.), *Ethics, the social sciences, and policy analysis.* New York: Plenum.

Neilsen, K. (1967). Problems of ethics. In *Encyclopedia of philosophy* (Vol. 3). New York: MacMillan.

Neuhaus, R. J. (1990, December). Joshing Richard Rorty. *First Things, 1*(8), 14-24.

Newton-Smith, W. (1981). *The rationality of science.* London: Routledge.

Nunnally, J. C. (1978). *Psychometric theory.* New York: McGraw-Hill.

Olinick, M. (1978). *An introduction to mathematical models in the social and life sciences.* Reading, MA: Addison-Wesley.

Phillips, D.C. (1992). *The social scientist's bestiary.* Oxford: Pergamon.

Popper, K. (1953). Three views concerning human knowledge. In H. D. Lewis (Ed.), *Contemporary British philosophy: Personal statements.* New York: Macmillan

Popper, K. (1968). *Conjectures and refutations..* New York: Harper Torchbooks.

Popper, K. (1976). The logic of the social sciences. In T. Adorno (Ed.), *Positivist dispute in German sociology.* New York: Harper Torchbooks.

Poundstone, W. (1992). *Prisoner's dilemma.* New York: Anchor Books.

Putnam, H. (1962). What theories are not. In E. Nagel, P. Suppes, & A. Tarski (Eds.), *Logic, methodology and philosophy of science: Proceedings of the 1960 International Congress.* Stanford: Stanford University Press.

Radelet, M. L. (1981). Racial characteristics and the imposition of the death penalty. *American Sociological Review, 46,* 918-927.

Rawlinson, G. (Trans.) (1932). *The history of Herodotus.* New York: Tudor Publishing.

Rein, M. (1983). Value-critical policy analysis. In D. Callahan & B. Jenners (Eds.), *Ethics, the social sciences, and policy analysis.* New York: Plenum.

Rorty, R. (1979). *Philosophy and the mirror of nature.* Princeton, NJ: Princeton University Press.

Rosenzweig, M. R., Bennett, E. L., & Diamond, M. C. (1972). Brain changes in response to experience. *Scientific American, 226,* 22-29.

Shapere, D. (1964). The structure of scientific revolutions. *Philosophical Review, 73,* 384-395.

Siegel, H. (1987). *Relativism refuted.* Dortrecht, The Netherlands: Reidel.

Sjoberg, G. (1975). Politics, ethics, and evaluation research. In E. Struening & M. Gutentag (Eds.), *Handbook of evaluation.* Beverly Hills, CA: Sage.

Skinner, B.F. (1971). *Beyond freedom and dignity.* New York: Alfred Knopf.

Sowell, T. (1995, February). Ethnicity and IQ. *The American Spectator, 28,* pp. 32-36.

Spencer, H. (1855). *The principles of psychology.* New York: D. Appleton and Company.

Spencer, H. (1949). *Essays on education.* London: Dent and Sons. (Original work published 1928)

Spirtes, P., Glymour, C., & Scheines, R. (1993). *Causation, prediction, and search. Lecture notes in statistics 81.* New York/Berlin: Springer-Verlag.

Suppes, F. (1974). *The structure of scientific theories.* Urbana: University of Illinois Press.

Suppes, P. (1970). *A probabilistic theory of causality.* Amsterdam: North-Holland Publishing.

Suppes, P., Krantz, D. H., Luce, R. D., & Tversky, A. (1989). *Foundations of measurements* (Vol. II). New York: Academic Press.

Tanur, J. M., Mostellar, F., Kruskal, W. H., Link, R. F., Pieters, R. S., & Rising, G. R. (Eds.). (1972). *Statistics: A guide to the unknown.* San Francisco: Holden-Day.

The MIT dictionary of modern economics. (1986). Cambridge: MIT Press.

Tieger, P. D., & Tieger, B. B. (1995). *Do what you are.* Boston: Little, Brown.

Tullock, G. (1959). Publication decisions and tests of significance: A comment. *Journal of the American Statistical Association, 54*(3), 593.

Turner, S. (1986). *The search for a methodology of social science.* Dordrecht, The Netherlands: D. Reidel.

von Neumann, J., & Morgenstern, O. (1937). *The theory of games and economic behavior.* Princeton, NJ: Princeton University Press.

von Neumann, J., & Morgenstern, O. (1946). *The theory of games and economic behavior* (2nd. ed.). Princeton, NJ: Princeton University Press.

von Neumann, J., & Morgenstern, O. (1953). *The theory of games and economic behavior* (3rd. ed.). Princeton, NJ: Princeton University Press.

Wallace, W. A. (Ed.). (1994). *Ethics in modeling.* Tarrytown, NY: Elvesier Science.

Warwick, D. P., & Pettigrew, T. F. (1983). Toward ethical guidelines for social science research in public policy. In D. Callahan & B. Jennings (Eds.), *Ethics, the social sciences, and policy analysis.* New York: Plenum.

Weiss, C. H. (1983). Ideology, interests, and information: The basis of policy positions. In D. Callahan & B. Jennings (Eds.), *Ethics, the social sciences, and policy analysis.* New York: Plenum.

Index

About the Authors

W. James Bradley teaches mathematics at Calvin College in Grand Rapids, Michigan. He is a 1964 graduate of the Massachusetts Institute of Technology and his PhD field was game theory (University of Rochester, 1974). He also has a master's degree in computer science (Rochester Institute of Technology, 1982). His research and publication interests include game theory, social choice theory, and ethical and social issues in computing. He has authored several textbooks in computer science and discrete mathematics.

Kurt C. Schaefer, a 1980 graduate (summa cum laude) of Bradley University, received his PhD from the University of Michigan (1984) in econometrics and economic development. He teaches economics at Calvin College in Grand Rapids, Michigan. His research and publication interests include U.S. welfare policy and the evaluation of third-world development projects. He has taught in a visiting university position in Budapest, Hungary, and has been involved with curriculum development in Moscow, Russia.